SPECTACULAR WINERIES
of New York

A CAPTIVATING TOUR OF ESTABLISHED, ESTATE AND BOUTIQUE WINERIES

Published by

PANACHE
PANACHE PARTNERS

Panache Partners, LLC
1424 Gables Court
Plano, TX 75075
469.246.6060
Fax: 469.246.6062
www.panache.com

Publishers: Brian G. Carabet and John A. Shand

Printed in Malaysia

Distributed by IPG
800.888.4741

PUBLISHER'S DATA

Spectacular Wineries of New York

Library of Congress Control Number: 2008920708

ISBN 13:   978-1-933415-65-9
ISBN 10:   1-933415-65-7

First Printing 2009

10 9 8 7 6 5 4 3 2 1

Previous Page: Raphael, *page 84*

Right: Photograph courtesy of Clark CSM Marketing Communications

All copy and photography published herein has been reviewed and
approved as free of any usage fees or rights and accurate by the individuals
and/or wineries included herein.

Panache Partners, LLC, is dedicated to the restoration and conservation of
the environment. Our *Spectacular Wineries* books are manufactured with
strict adherence to an environmental management system in accordance
with ISO 14001 standards, including the use of paper from mills certified
to derive their products from environmentally managed forests. We are
committed to continued investigation of alternative paper products and
environmentally responsible manufacturing processes to ensure the
preservation of our fragile planet.

SPECTACULAR WINERIES
of New York

A CAPTIVATING TOUR OF ESTABLISHED, ESTATE AND BOUTIQUE WINERIES

Vetter Vineyards Winery, *page 304*

T he New York wine industry is experiencing an exciting renaissance. As one of the oldest winegrowing states, New York claims the first recorded vintage, which appeared in 1839. From that point, the region continued to grow into one of the largest wine-producers until Prohibition devastated the industry nationwide.

After repeal, New York's industry recovered very slowly due to the understandable caution of investors. The first wave of resurgence began with the Farm Winery Act of 1976, a state law that encouraged the creation of local wine business. At that time, New York had 19 wineries; today there are more than 230. The 1985 creation of the New York Wine & Grape Foundation for promotion and research further accelerated the growth rate: more than three-quarters of New York's wineries have opened since then.

Secondly, and equally important, vineyard developments took place. Historically New York grew only Vitis labrusca grapes, or Native American, such as Concord and Niagara, possessing fruity aroma and flavors. In the years following repeal, French-American varieties like baco noir and seyval blanc were planted, combining the best of both worlds: the winter hardiness of native varieties with the more sophisticated taste profile of European wines.

The third wave involved Vitis vinifera grapes, traditional European varieties such as pinot noir and riesling, introduced by two European immigrants. France's Charles Fournier and Russia's Dr. Konstantin Frank sparked the vinifera revolution, bringing viticultural advancements to the United States. Today, the vast majority of New York wineries produce vinifera wines along with a selection of French-American and Native American selections to satisfy every consumer taste.

New York is vibrant and exciting because of its diversity—people, cultures and customs. And its wine industry shares the same virtue, with an array of types and styles, the unique growing regions, and the people who share a passion for wine. Wine is an art form. It is born of the earth, raised by farmers and shaped by winemakers into a unique mosaic of toil, decisions and care. Vineyards, vintages and artistry are reflected in each bottle.

Art and aesthetics overlap into the wine industry, with many tasting rooms showcasing paintings and sculpture at special events or as part of the overall ambience. Crafting the wine extends beyond the glass to the physical architecture of the winery. New York has some of the country's oldest, most historic wineries amongst modern, state-of-the-art facilities.

This elegant book provides a visual journey through the artistry of the New York wine industry. The places, people and philosophies depicted on these pages are a window into the passion that unites the state's diversity. I hope you will share this book with others while enjoying a glass of New York wine, and pay a visit to the region for a tasteful experience.

Jim Trezise
President, New York Wine & Grape Foundation

Introduction

New York Wine & Culinary Center

Photograph courtesy of New York Wine & Culinary Center

Designed to engage, excite and inspire the people of New York—and the world—in a celebration of the state's culinary contributions, the New York Wine & Culinary Center is an educational and experiential opening to the state's incredible wine and food industries.

Since the center opened in June 2006, it has hosted individuals and groups who come to taste and learn about the best New York has to offer. The center houses an expansive tasting room, restaurant, retail shop, demonstration theater, hands-on gourmet kitchen, exhibition area and private dining room. Programs include cooking and wine seminars for consumers, professionals and industry people; educational programs; food and wine tours; exhibitions; and private parties.

The New York Wine & Culinary Center views itself as a place to whet the appetite—to introduce visitors to the diversity of New York, piquing their curiosity about what they might discover upon further investigation; and to provide them with the knowledge to explore New York's world of wine and food.

While the center is located in New York's wine country, the Finger Lakes, you can virtually visit every region by enjoying a statewide, rotating wine list. Sample the great wines of New York with luscious dishes prepared with local ingredients...it is truly a gateway to the bounty of New York agriculture.

Photographs courtesy of New York Wine & Culinary Center

Penguin Bay Winery and Champagne House, *page 234*

Photograph courtesy of Clark CSM Marketing Communications

From the Publisher

What comes to mind when you hear the words New York? The name probably doesn't conjure up images of vast vineyards and endless glasses of wine. Instead, visions of a bustling city, full of busy people and Metro trains appear. But the vintners outside of the urban sprawl have begun to change that, one bottle at a time. As the country's third largest grape-producing state with five distinct growing regions, New York has so much more to offer the culinary world than just its big city appeal and Manhattan restaurants. A rich wine culture exists, gaining momentum and promising national and international success for the regions. The Farm Winery Act of 1976 launched the industry, deregulating the state's wine market and allowing viticultural commerce to thrive. Winemakers could now sell their products to individuals and restaurants instead of working through a distributor—typically a costly and lengthy process. The new legislation gave smaller wineries a fighting chance against the state's major sellers and let quality become the barometer to measuring a successful product.

On the shores of Long Island, the vineyards have the benefit of the Atlantic Ocean's moderating forces; ocean wind keeps the vines cool in the summer and the water provides insulation through the cold months of winter. With such a dynamic climate and wineries like Pindar Vineyards, Castello di Borghese and Wölffer Estate, Long Island produces everything from cabernet sauvignon to tocai friulano. Due west, the Hudson River Valley claims the title as the first place in America to plant vineyards, in addition to having the oldest continuously operating winery in the country—Brotherhood Winery. Hudson Valley wines made from classic European varieties, including their own seyval blanc, blended with a choice of vignoles, vidal or Cayuga white, are well adapted to growing conditions and combine to produce a well balanced wine called Hudson Heritage White. Driving an hour and half through New York, you may be surprised by the natural beauty of the area and its many historic sites.

Situated in the western-central portion of Upstate New York, the Finger Lakes region boasts more than 100 wineries and 50-plus varietals. Annual production is in excess of 100 million bottles. It's like stepping back in time. No hurried people, no fast food, just pure, clean scenery. Every glance reveals lush vineyards or picturesque lakes—so pure that the untreated water is fit to drink. Once-present glaciers left the shores with traces of shale, slate and strong deposits of clay that become evident in the wine bottle. Master winemakers like Dr. Konstantin Frank and Hermann J. Weimer have paved the way for the region's future, helping to expand the area to roughly 11,000 planted acres.

Lake Erie and Niagara have become the state's rising stars of wine. Niagara Escarpment is minutes from Niagara Falls—a drive that winds around beautiful vistas of old farmlands and rural county life. This is the perfect way to spend a relaxing afternoon. Lake Erie is best known for its vinifera, ice wines, fruit wines and specialty wines like brandies and ports. Vineyard grapes and hauntingly calm waters give way to winter's eventual freeze, when white caps and infinite ice provide a stunning backdrop. The locals, however, manage to stay warm and welcoming. A home-cooked meal with the perfect bottle of wine is never far. Each region plays host with the culinary delights of bed and breakfasts while offering a landscape that holds visitors in awe, no matter the season. Try the riesling, seyval blanc, chardonnay, pinot noir, sparkling wines and cabernet sauvignon, among others. You'll have a new friend in the cellar before you know it.

Cheers,

Kathryn Newell

Regional Publisher

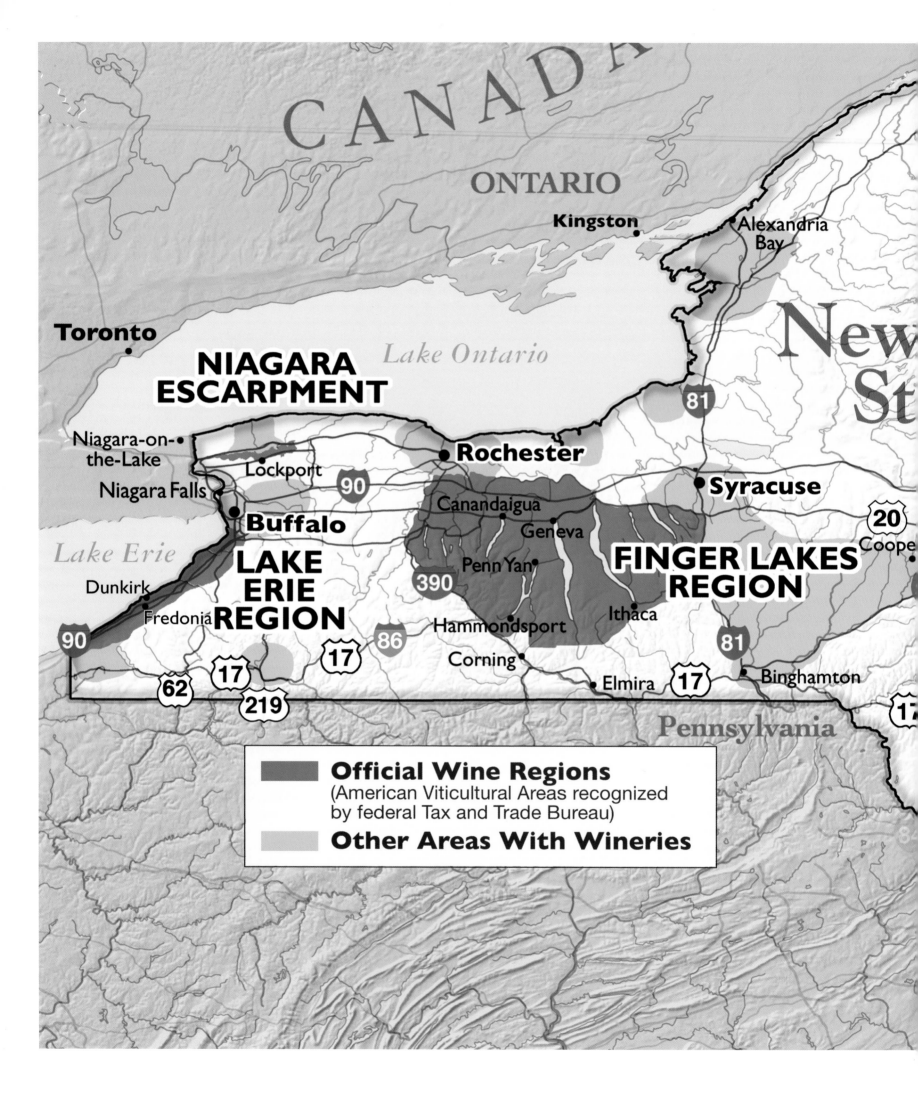

CANADA

ONTARIO

Kingston

• Alexandria Bay

Toronto

Lake Ontario

Ne
St

New
St

NIAGARA
ESCARPMENT

Niagara-on-the-Lake

Rochester

Syracuse

Lockport

90

Canandaigua

20

Coope

Niagara Falls

Geneva

Buffalo

390

Penn Yan

FINGER LAKES
REGION

Lake Erie

LAKE
ERIE
REGION

Dunkirk

Ithaca

Fredonia

86

Hammondsport

81

90

17

Corning

Binghamton

62

17

Elmira

17

219

Pennsylvania

17

Official Wine Regions
(American Viticultural Areas recognized
by federal Tax and Trade Bureau)
Other Areas With Wineries

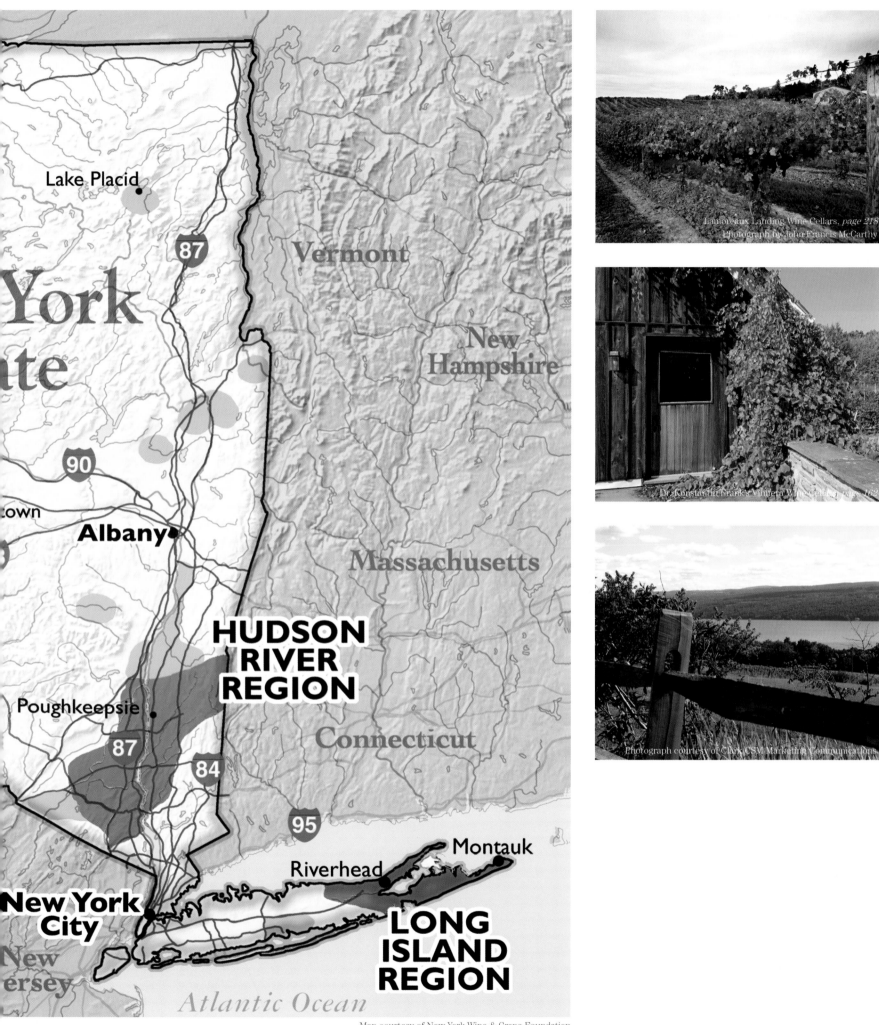

Lake Placid

87

Vermont

New York State

90

Albany

Massachusetts

New Hampshire

HUDSON RIVER REGION

Poughkeepsie

87

84

Connecticut

95

New York City

Riverhead

Montauk

LONG ISLAND REGION

New Jersey

Atlantic Ocean

Lamoreaux Landing Wine Cellars, *page 218*
Photograph by John Francis McCarthy

Dr. Konstantin Frank's Vinifera Wine Cellars, *page 162*

Photograph courtesy of Clark CSM Marketing Communications

Map courtesy of New York Wine & Grape Foundation

Table of Contents

Long Island

Hudson Valley

Finger Lakes

Ventosa Vineyards, *page 258*

Niagara

Erie

Raphael, *page 84*

Comtesse Thérèse, *page 36*

Long Island

Bedell Cellars

Cutchogue

It is hard to believe that one of the most highly regarded wineries in the eastern United States began with the hobby of one man—Kip Bedell's interest in winemaking. He picked up the craft in the 1970s without realizing just how far-reaching its effects would be. At that time, the wine world of New York was in its infancy but had begun to gain some solid recognition for its forging pursuits, giving Kip an investigative incentive for land purchase in the North Fork.

Kip and his wife Susan discovered David's Farm, a 50-acre plot that they wanted to call their own. The Cutchogue land was being used for potato fields at the time, but the couple saw its hidden potential. Flat land, cool summer nights and sandy soil convinced the two that they could make this work. Regularly making the long commute to the property, the Bedells put their first vines into the ground with the help of a 1951 Ford V8 pick-up truck and a handful of dedicated friends. In a 10-year period, seven acres of vines were tended to and so well kept that 1986 saw a gold medal from the *Dallas Morning News* competition go to the Chardonnay Reserve. This affirmation of quality work gave the growers the boost they needed, pushing the fruit-bearing acreage count up to 19 and the next year's case production up to 3,000. A solid foundation was built.

Seeing the North Fork's promise, businessman and movie mogul Michael Lynne decided that with such a high-quality production and an ideal location, a New York winery would be a rewarding purchase. He had already bought Corey Creek Vineyard and wanted to add a sophisticated practice with high prospective values, leading him to Bedell Cellars.

Top Left: Film executive, wine enthusiast and native New Yorker, Michael Lynne owns both Bedell Cellars and Corey Creek Vineyard.
Photograph courtesy of New Line Cinema

Bottom Left: Top cuvées include Gallery White, Musée Red and the Estate Merlot.

Facing Page: Young syrah vines sit behind sweet-scented lavender.

Formerly a partner with an entertainment law firm and co-chairman and co-CEO of New Line Cinema, Michael knows a successful business venture when he sees one. What started as an independent film company is now at the forefront of the entertainment industry, speaking volumes about Michael's corporate abilities. Achieving 11 Academy Awards, the Lord of the Rings Trilogy—the most successful film franchise in history—was made with Michael as the executive producer. A lover of not only film, but fine arts as a whole, Michael sits on the board of directors at the Museum of Modern Art, the American Museum of the Moving Image and other non-profit organizations.

With Michael's impressive record of success, Kip and Susan trusted the future of Bedell in his hands. They sold the cellars in 2000 but remain heavily involved, with Kip on board as the winemaker emeritus. Michael has taken the winery to new heights, bringing in his love of fine arts and extending its reputation to make the name synonymous with refinement and taste.

Top Right: Corey Creek Vineyard sits in Southold, on the northeastern tip of Long Island's North Fork.

Bottom Right: Newly planted Dijon-clone chardonnay vines will make world-class bottles of wine.

Facing Page: The view from the Corey Creek tasting room is especially lush and idyllic, keeping visitors returning time and again.

Previous Pages: The tasting pavilion is frequently the scene for live music and outdoor wine sampling.

Bedell Cellars now bottles wines from the fields in its own backyard plus the Wells Road and Corey Creek Vineyard. Touted as one of the region's strongest producers of fine chardonnay and merlot, the winery has recently—and increasingly—garnered attention for its blends. Aggressively pursuing the art of crafting blends, the use of acclaimed chardonnay and merlot grapes as foundations for these concoctions is no surprise. The Taste Series features lines of red and white combinations; the Taste Red mixes cabernet sauvignon, cabernet franc and syrah with a merlot base. Resulting in a complex wine, the nose expresses ripe black fruit, vanilla and toast, with a subtle earthiness. For the Taste White, aromatic riesling, viognier and gewürztraminer come together with a chardonnay base to create a unique and compelling swirl of fruit and floral flavors. Anyone daunted by complicated wines will be pleased to try the First Crush line. Produced in steel tanks as opposed to oak barrels, the First Crush white wines bring together chardonnay and viognier and the First Crush red mingles cabernet franc and merlot. Using the steel tanks keeps the spirits light and crisp, making them a welcome guest at any dinner table and a friend of everyday foods like pizza, sushi and grilled meats or vegetables.

Right: Corey Creek Vineyard's tasting room is open and airy, yet has the same inviting warmth as Bedell Cellars.

Facing Page Top: The tasting room at Bedell Cellars is modern and minimalist in design.

Facing Page Bottom Left: A mezzanine level in the tasting room allows guests to sit down and enjoy each others' company over a glass of wine.

Facing Page Bottom Right: Bedell Cellars offers a warm atmosphere in a contemporary setting—perfect for sampling the winery's selections.

Two master blends have been distinguished above the rest, Gallery and Museé. The Gallery offers a fine mix of top-tier chardonnay, sauvignon blanc and viognier, with an outcome that transcends individual grape varieties to invent a powerful combination. Smooth and long in the mouth, Museé is from the 2005 vintage and delivers an impressive cross of merlot and cabernet sauvignon. Hailed as the winery's finest, the flavors of deep-hued fruits are polished and elegant.

Although the wine seems to effortlessly appear on dinner tables, there is a network of effort that goes on behind the scenes. At Bedell, a core group works closely to ensure the quality of the wine, beginning with Trent Preszler. Studies in botany at the University of Edinburgh and a master's degree in agricultural economics from Cornell mixed with years of management experience in the field has put Trent where he is today as the chief operating officer. Jim

Silver, senior vice-president of sales and marketing, has upward of two decades in the food and beverage business under his belt. His diverse background brings a great deal of perspective to the table, holding a culinary and business degree from Walnut Hill College in Philadelphia plus working for hotel groups and vineyards in France, Spain and Napa Valley.

Above: Spectacular landscaping adds to the winery's exterior—almost as distracting as the surrounding vineyards.

Right: Various specimens of plants can be found on the cellars' grounds, framing the tasting room.

Facing Page Top: A copper-covered tasting bar grabs the attention of wine enthusiasts as they arrive for a glass.

Facing Page Bottom: During fermentation, the barrel room is filled with the sights, sounds and smells of the winemaking process.

A defining dimension to the company, Pascal Marty works with Bedell as the consulting winemaker. Pascal studied enology at the Institute of Bordeaux and then went on to serve as the director of winemaking for the Baron Philippe de Rothschild. His role aided in the vast expansion of the company launching joint ventures with Robert Mondavi's Opus One in California and Concha y Toro's Vina Almaviva in Chile. As co-general manager of Vina Almaviva, Pascal revitalized the vineyards and has consequently earned consistent top ratings amongst Chilean wines. Pascal offers his expertise to a few select wineries in the world, Bedell being one of the only three in North America.

As lead winemaker, Kelly Urbanik plays a key role in propelling the winery's drive for perfection, and wine critics are sure to take notice. Kelly grew up in St. Helena, California, with a close connection to a vintner's lifestyle. She received her Bachelor of Science in viticulture

and enology from UC Davis and worked the 2003 harvest at Maison Louis Jadot. As the first woman winemaker in the Long Island wine trade, she holds a distinguished place on the team.

Constantly progressive, Bedell winery has a knack for blending classic and contemporary. A potato barn from 1919 for example, has been renovated to use as winemaking space. State-of-the-art equipment is hidden by buildings that would have made Norman Rockwell proud—vaulted, barn-style facilities show off great American porches that look out to apple orchards, lavender fields and sweeping greens. A Manhattan interior designer has combined contemporary decor with the setting and included a highly valued collection of artwork in the

Above: The outdoor pavilion is often the host of summer weddings and special events.

Facing Page: Merlot vines absorb the sun, enhancing the fruit's flavors.

winery's ambience. Staying in cue with Michael's penchant for modern art, world renowned contemporary artists Eric Fischl, Barbara Kruger, Ross Bleckner, Chuck Close and April Gornik have brought their artistic talents to the Bedell family, placing their work on select bottles. The juxtaposition of traditional and modern has made the winery a perfect selection for weddings and special events, offering the best of both worlds while providing remarkable wines.

WINE & FARE

Bedell Musée
(merlot, cabernet sauvignon, petit verdot)

Pair with luxurious and textural foods; simple oven-roasted rack of lamb, seasoned lightly with salt, pepper and fresh thyme or rosemary, cooked no further than medium-rare; but no overpowering flavors.

Bedell Gallery
(chardonnay, sauvignon blanc, viognier)

Pair with fillet of turbot, crusted with fresh herbs and roasted on a cedar plank; grilled split lobster or langoustines, painted with butter, sea salt and white pepper; classic Italian pot-roasted chicken with root vegetables, baby potatoes, 20 cloves of garlic and fresh rosemary sprigs; and rich, intense foods that are not too spicy.

Taste Red

Pair with pork tenderloin, lightly dusted with Cajun seasoning; leg of lamb studded with garlic and grilled; London broil rubbed with a dry marinade of ginger, pepper, mace and crushed herbs.

First Crush White
(chardonnay, viognier)

Pair with light foods and appetizers; hors d'oeuvres like classic clams casino spiced up with jalapenos or chorizos, grilled over smoky mesquite; white-fleshed fish steamed with vegetables and herbs, or grilled with olive oil and sea salt.

Tastings
Open to the public daily, year-round

Castello di Borghese
Vineyard and Winery

Cutchogue

Living the life of a modern-day prince or princess is not as easy as people may think. Bringing their ninth-century, aristocratic roots to life, Marco and Ann Marie Borghese own and operate Castello di Borghese Vineyard on Long Island. They embody the noble life, infusing it into every event, every interaction and every bottle of wine. Their castle—or *castello*—is a testament to the hard work and passion it has taken to reach this point.

Living *la dolce vita*, Marco spent his young years on a self-sustaining farm outside of Florence. The thousands of acres that comprised the farm were a snapshot of Italy's most admirable qualities—fertile, rolling earth and endless skies. When Marco left the motherland for big-city America, his life as a businessman eventually began to lack a certain something. His "back to basics" calling brought the couple to purchase a landmark winery in 1999, where he watched his three children flourish in an environment that mirrored his upbringing.

At the time, the less-than-perfect condition of the winery presented a challenge to the Borgheses. Not only did they have a great deal of physical work to do in order to revitalize the land and its structures, but spreading the word of their new venture would be an undertaking, as well. Ann Marie's cultured background allowed her to put a new spin on the rural life of a winery. She honed her business skills at her boutique jewelry shop in Philadelphia, preparing for the social, outgoing nature of the wine industry. Her mostly-pro bono work was centered around museum and gallery functions, providing the perfect background to create an ambience of elegant entertainment at the vineyard.

Top Left: Redefining the public concept of royalty, Princess Ann Marie and Prince Marco Borghese have devoted endless hours to their passion for wine.

Middle Left: Just as it appears in the countryside of Italy, the Borghese crest adorns a wooden gift box.
Photograph by Richard Ritter

Bottom Left: Bunch by bunch, each harvest brings a taste of the year's labor.

Facing Page: The Meritage-Bordeaux blend and merlot reserve saw particularly good years from 2000 to 2003.
Photograph by Richard Ritter

In a successful effort to put the family's name on the wine map, Ann Marie began doing what she knew how to do best: she threw parties worthy of a princess. Operas, balls, art viewings and poetry readings began to fill the winery's date-book—benefiting charities and cueing people in on Ann Marie's social savvy and event know-how. Initially received with uncertainty, the galas were a hit. Castello di Borghese soon became a cultural destination, entertaining visitors with wine, food and fine arts.

A gracious high-ceiling barn previously used as a holding room was included on the historic property; Ann Marie saw an opportunity. She cleared out the old to make room for the new and utilized the space to hold her first opera, La Bohème. The event turned out better than anyone had expected and immediately set the bar to the Borghese standard. Guests entered into a world that slowed down the usual, aggressive pace of city living and let the finer things in life receive the attention they deserved.

The Borghese family wants visitors to appreciate nature's bounty and understand what it means to live the Italian noble life—quiet, slow, internal. As blessed stewards of the land, they remain connected to the earth and urge others to try a slice of life from a bygone era. The Old World had serfs on horseback, traveling from artisan to artisan to pick up groceries for the evening feast. Freshly hunted game, cheeses, herbs and honey were all gathered. Food was hand-crafted and dictated daily activities; people were both spiritually and physically closer to the land. Because Marco's early life held so many of these elements, the Borgheses are governed by this pervasive philosophy and hope to transpose these values to guests—at least for the duration of their visit.

Above: A modern-day palace for the family, the Borgheses' *castello* sits on the vineyards.
Photograph by William L. Carpenter

Right: Careful wine pairing takes place in the Borghese dining room.
Photograph by Ann Marie Borghese

Facing Page Top: A 1951 farm truck works perfectly to announce the signature red, pinot noir.

Facing Page Bottom: Unabashedly devoted to Ann Marie and the Borghese family, Brix—a bracco Italiano—found happiness at the winery after his rescue from a Southern dog shelter.
Photograph by Paula Daniel

The vineyards are a mixture of old and new vines, beginning with the first planting in 1973; varietals include sauvignon blanc, chardonnay, merlot, cabernet franc and pinot noir. Yielding wines with an open appeal, the grape flavors refrain from being overly esoteric on the palate and can be enjoyed by both the novice and the connoisseur. Marco constantly monitors the grapes' progression, spending a great deal of his time in the fields and the cellar. With a predominant focus on pinot noir grapes, this award-winning wine has become a signature and showcases the winemaking talent of the Borghese family. Marco's culinary skills help ensure that the vines deliver a food-friendly result. The couple encourages tasters to explore local cuisine, consequently heightening the appreciation of the experience. Events at the *castello* reflect their advice on taking advantage of regional bounty, which includes gourmet demonstrations, olive oil tastings with Italian-imported oil from a family estate and wine-accompanied dessert tastings.

Top Left: Once a strawberry bin and a chicken coop, the property's small wooden buildings have long since housed farming equipment.

Middle Left: From the oldest vines on Long Island, the Founder's Field Sauvignon Blanc is the signature white wine.
Photograph © Kevin Ferris

Bottom Left: Exhibiting power and grace, the wines mature to their full potential in French barrels.

Facing Page: Full of life and color, the vines indicate when they are ready for gathering.

BORGHESE

From noble Italian agricultural roots to urban living, Castello di Borghese Vineyard has helped the family come full circle since taking over as proprietors of Long Island's founding vineyard. Under the land's watch, each member of the family has grown and thrived, giving great significance to each passing year. With so many blessings and fortunes, they are more than pleased to share their home with visitors, keeping the winery open year-round for tours and tastings. Thankful for this lifestyle and opportunity, Marco and Ann Marie's eyes are always open for progression and continuation—hoping that everyone seizes the chance to realize a dream, just as they have.

WINE & FARE

Pinot Noir Reserve

Pair with veal casa rustica—lightly breaded and pan-fried cutlets—served alongside insalata Caprese with garlic and finely cut red onions.

Sauvignon Blanc Founder's Field

Pair with cayenne-spiced savory truffles; heirloom tomato, pepper cress and goat cheese fritters with verjus and virgin olive oil; or pan-seared scallops and shrimp with fricassee of oyster mushrooms and leeks.

Allegra Dessert Wine

Pair with rich chocolate truffles; or sweet peach and raspberry tart with vanilla-bean gelato and warm caramel.

Merlot

Pair with Tuscan-grilled wild salmon topped with a caper and kalamata olive relish; peppery buffalo fillet mignon in a red wine reduction; eggplant caponata bruschetti with goat cheese; or cinnamon-scented Italian fudge cake.

Tastings

Open to the public daily, seasonally

Comtesse Thérèse

Aquebogue

When the word winemaker first crossed attorney Theresa Dilworth's mind, she pictured herself spending leisurely hours of retirement in the vineyards—30 years in the future. On a small scale, she had always loved making homemade beer, wine and soda for entertaining. It seemed like a perfect hobby to dive into—the opportunity just came a little sooner than she expected.

She purchased residential land in Mattituck, New York, for a country retreat. In a two-year period, Theresa and her husband Mineo "Sammy" Shimura worked to clear brush and trees, build a home and construct a road for access to the outside world. As she discovered the magnificent wine region that surrounded her, it seemed only natural to take her hobby to the next level. The discussion of opening a winery came up, with friends offering a share of the down payment. Those friends soon became business partners with a total of 40 acres for potential vineyard space. Under the counsel of a specialist from the University of Bordeaux, the team agreed that only the most suitable land should be used to plant the vinifera vines and sold the remaining acreage to a neighboring vegetable farmer. They now grow varietals with 70 percent of the crop as cabernet sauvignon. It is a grape that ripens later in the season with a slow development of tannins. This imparts a more complex, intense flavor that heightens its promise as a winning wine.

Maintaining a job in the city and fulfilling the role as head winemaker quickly proved to be exhausting; Theresa turned to Sammy for help. Sammy had spent his career in the Japanese and American steel industry as a chairman and CEO, which afforded him little to no knowledge of viticulture. His initial reluctance melted away however, when he enrolled in a sommelier course in the area. The top-notch scores he received beat

Top Left: In vine rows less than five feet apart in the estate's Le Clos Thérèse, Mineo Shimura and Theresa Dilworth spend a great deal of time with the cabernet sauvignon.

Bottom Left: A selection of wines line up inside the multi-vineyard tasting room—the only one on Long Island of its kind. Wines from Comtesse Thérèse and several other limited production, boutique vineyards appear.

Facing Page: Renovated to become a wine tasting room and bistro, the building dates back to the 1830s. Comtesse Thérèse wines grace the menu, as well as local eastern Long Island foods.

everyone in the class and he discovered a hidden passion. Sammy now spends seven days a week managing and farming Le Clos Thérèse—a small, enclosed vineyard. He practices high-density planting: a method that places 2,500 vines on each acre. The technique results in a greater amount of hand work and the use of specialized equipment, making it a more expensive method. Sammy and Theresa think the cost is worth the benefit, affording results that would please vintners of premier sites in Burgundy and Bordeaux. Theresa's grandmother's family is from Alsace, where generations ago they owned vineyards.

Husband and wife Bernard and Lisa Julian Cannac offer their skills and taste buds to Comtesse Thérèse, with Bernard serving as the consultant winemaker and Lisa as the assistant winemaker. Frenchman Bernard has a repertoire with years of work in the industry and of formal enology studies, plus a family-run winery in the south of France. Lisa is the former lab director of Premium Wine Group and ensures that the wine is placed in the right markets. Together, these four enthusiasts taste each harvest and develop blends, relying on one another's palates and opinions.

Their good taste and distinctive methods have put forth acclaimed wines. Comtesse Thérèse uses international wood species during barrel-aging to give the wine its unique tasting notes. Since Eastern Europe had provided barrels for France until the onset of World War I, it seemed like a good idea to rehash the subtleties of wine that worked. It has proved just as effective as it was for France a century ago. The Comtesse Thérèse Hungarian Oak Merlot was named 2004's best merlot at the New York Food and Wine Classic. A round, medium-bodied wine, it exhibits violet, black pepper and a hint of cloves on the tongue. The Hungarian oak barreling gives it a perfect spiciness that makes it stand out from other merlots. For the chardonnay bottlings, Russian oak has been used to avoid an over-oaky flavor. The wood is subtle, with floral and honey notes; the nose is clean, giving off eucalyptus, citrus and toasted walnuts. Keep an eye out for upcoming wood varieties— Theresa is constantly looking for new species to try.

Above Left: Founded in 2003, the 1860s general store-turned-tasting room saw Comtesse Thérèse become operator in July 2006.

Above Right: The estate vineyard sees the merlot bud break in late April, when the grape leaves first emerge after winter dormancy.

Facing Page: When harvest time arrives, cabernet sauvignon grapes show deep color, uniform shape and the promise of a perfect vintage.

As if Theresa did not have enough on her plate, she has definite plans to grow the winery. She has purchased a nearby parcel of land with her parents to plant a second vineyard, Las Côtes, giving them the same enjoyment that she and her husband receive from spending time on the land while trying some new varietals such as syrah, sauvignon blanc and malbec. Her successful take-over of a cooperative Long Island tasting room has spawned the urge to open another one, this time closer to the vineyards. The prospective building is a historic home from the 1830s, guaranteed to add charm to an already picturesque setting.

Comtesse Thérèse

WINE & FARE

Traditional Merlot
Pair with grilled or roast lamb, beef, steak or holiday turkey.

Cabernet Sauvignon Reserve
Pair with beef, lamb and any variety of mushrooms.

Blanc de Noir
Pair with charcuterie, omelets and quiches, Asian cuisine, and vanilla ice cream.

Russian Oak Chardonnay
Pair with shellfish, halibut, chicken salad or Caesar salad.

Tastings
Not currently open to the public

Duck Walk Vineyards

Water Mill

I f F. Scott Fitzgerald stated a truth in his journals when he wrote "action is character," then Dr. Herodotus Damianos is, indeed, full of character. Packed with education and pursuit, the life of Herodotus, or Dr. Dan, has remained perpetually active with a long list of life's most exciting successes to prove it.

Born in Manhattan to a Greek family, Herodotus spent his young life in the Bronx. And although his mother died at an early age, she left an impression that only a mother can, giving her son a prophetic name: Dyonisius, Greek god of wine. As a lover of books, chronicles and narratives, his father changed his son's name to Herodotus, deeming it more appropriate for a child that would likely resemble him. But neither of his parents could predict the dynamic path Dr. Dan chose for himself. While studying at New York University to become a teacher, Dr. Dan put his education on hold to serve in the Korean War. Although his duty to the country was an unplanned departure, Dr. Dan continued schooling toward his PhD at Columbia upon his return. But once he decided to become a physician, his mind was made up; the young graduate traveled to the University of Bologna in Italy for medical school. Like anyone who spends an extended period of time in the Mediterranean, Dr. Dan developed an appreciation of wine and land—an experience that made him feel not-so-far removed from the family vineyard in Olympia.

Top Left: Alexandar and Lacy stand proudly at Duck Walk North.

Middle Left: Duck Walk South vineyards remain under meticulous care since the winery opened in 1994.

Bottom Left: Duck Walk wines include Pinot Grigio, Aphrodite, Blueberry Port and Boysenberry.

Facing Page: The winery is a well-known name in South Hampton.
Photograph by Ralph Pugliese, Jr.

Now, with a handful of hard-earned degrees, five children, and more than three decades as a private practice internist, Dr. Dan can also claim his throne as the king of Long Island wine. Owning 550 acres of the region's finest grapes, the head of the Damianos family pushed for recognition when there simply was none to be found. The phrase "Long Island wine" was unheard of in the 1960s when his entrepreneurial ideas sprouted. But make no mistake—establishing the region's wine trade was no accident. Dr. Dan saw an area that begged for expansion, first coming across fledgling vines in a lot near his first home in Stony Brook. He saw the big picture, which made him willing to invest money, equipment and at least 80 hours of his time each week to reach his vision.

Opening 15 years after Pindar, Duck Walk Vineyards South Hampton and Duck Walk Vineyards North operate under the careful eye of Alexander, the oldest of the Damianos children named after Alexander the Great. Two MBAs and an innate love of viticulture give Alexander the perfect mix of traits to perpetuate Duck Walk's success, sitting on the South Fork of Long Island in Water Mill.

Above: Duck Walk North has a VIP room that is perfect for meetings, conferences and gatherings.

Facing Page: The South Hampton tasting room lets visitors browse through selections.

Top: Patio seating at Duck Walk North overlooks the vineyards—a perfect accompaniment to a glass of wine.

Bottom: Row by row, the vineyards show off Long Island's natural charm—vivid, green and welcoming.

Top: Warm and humble, the front entrance hints at the personality of the winery.

Bottom: Surrounded by fall foliage and lush ground, the winery seems to fit perfectly into the landscape.

A milestone on the Hamptons' countryside, Duck Walk spreads over 130 acres of grapes and produces upward of 25,000 cases annually. Modeled after a Normandy château, the winery has garnered more silver, gold and double gold medals than any vintner could ever hope for. Pulling in prizes from San Diego, Florida, the Pacific Rim and multiple international contests, the winery's achievements include gold for the vidal blanc and chardonnay in the American Wine Society competition. Fans are hard-pressed to find a wine that has not earned recognition over the years, ranging from success with everything from the boysenberry wine to the cabernet sauvignon.

Embodying the class and good taste of Long Island, Duck Walk labels feature the high-rolling scenes from Jazz Age youths—picture Daisy Buchanan in all her leisure. Gatsby Red, a medium-bodied, semi-sweet blend of cabernet sauvignon, merlot and other varietals, shows off an elegant young woman donned in a red cloche hat and pearls in front of an American mansion and a Rolls Royce. And Art Deco fashion shots appear on other selections, like the merlot and cabernet sauvignon reserve, giving a peek into the haute couture of the Roaring '20s.

Right: The fermentation room gives off a rich smell—a combination of the grapes, alcohol and wood barrels.

Facing Page: A view of the vineyards alone is worth a trip to New York.

Truth be told, the best way to learn about Duck Walk Vineyards is from Dr. Dan himself. With all of the engaging qualities of a well-versed professor, the patriarch of Damianos wine can be found giving tours and educating visitors, often incognito.

WINE & FARE

Pinot Noir
Pair with grilled wild striped bass with fresh herbs, asparagus salad with roasted red peppers and goat cheese or braised short ribs with whole grain mustard.

Vidal Ice
Pair with Granny Smith and brown butter custard tart, walnut-date toffee cake and sweetened whipped cream or apple-pecan crisp.

Windmill Red
Accompanies crab cakes dipped in cayenne-spiced mayonnaise, tandoori lamb or mozzarella and vegetable panini.

Tastings
Open to the public daily, year-round

Jason's Vineyard

Jamesport

As the Greek legend goes, Jason, the mythological hero who rallied the Argonauts and rightfully deserved the rule of Thessaly, received his education from the centaur Chiron. Known for his comprehensive intelligence in medicine and observance of social propriety, Chiron educated Jason on a variety of subjects, including the intricacies of plant life and the civilized arts. And although Jason Damianos—owner of Jason's Vineyard—lives on Long Island in the 21st century, far from the roots of Western civilization, he shares more in common with his Greek namesake than just a moniker.

Both of Mediterranean descent, the men hold a cultural connection that has always been apparent in the Damianos household. His parents have celebrated their lineage, paying homage to poets, gods and lore by using traditional names for all five of their children. And just as the Jason of ancient times had a mentor, Jason Damianos had the guiding hand of his father, Dr. Herodotus. Like Chiron, Herodotus, or Dr. Dan as he is known, has extensive knowledge in both medicine and agriculture; he is a licensed internist and has spent nearly 30 years growing grapes and making wine.

Top Left: Jason Damianos owns the namesake winery and serves as the winemaker.

Bottom Left: The good ship Argo, which Jason sailed in search of the golden fleece, symbolizes the history of the winery's, and the founder's, name.

Facing Page: Surrounded by Merlot vines in Jamesport, the winery was built in 2008.
Photograph by Ralph Pugliese, Jr.

Jason's Vineyard sits on Jamesport on the north fork of Long Island, encompassing a 20-acre space. After receiving a bachelor of science degree in business administration from the University of Hartford, Jason received a second bachelor's degree in enology from the California State University at Fresno, acquiring honors and accolades for his work including the coveted Merit award given to one outstanding enology student per year. Continuing his studies, he attended the University of Bordeaux—a Mecca for wine academics—and worked in renowned regions of the Medoc, Premieres Cotes de Bordeaux,

Loupiac and Cadillac. With an education like this, high-quality vines were inevitably in Jason's future. Very little space between the rows promises superior fruit, the Long Island vineyard flourishes with the finest French clones: chardonnay, merlot, cabernet sauvignon, malbec and cabernet franc.

Above & Facing Page: In 1997 Jason's Vineyard was laser planted, in one-by-two meter sections. Here, chardonnay vines are well protected from attack by birds.

Jason has perfected a Meritage blend that has received industry attention since its first vintage. A combination of merlot, cabernet franc and cabernet sauvignon ages in French oak to create a complex wine filled with ripe fruit, rich tannins and a touch of earthiness. The wine possesses the virtue of versatility; it can easily be served immediately or held to mature for future drinking. Like all of the selections on Jason's wine list, the Meritage blend reflects the thought, care and skill that appears in every bottle.

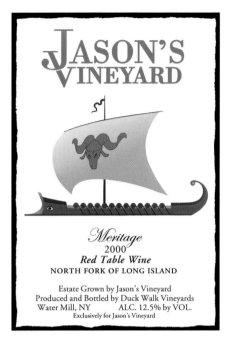

JASON'S VINEYARD

Meritage
2000
Red Table Wine
NORTH FORK OF LONG ISLAND

Estate Grown by Jason's Vineyard
Produced and Bottled by Duck Walk Vineyards
Water Mill, NY   ALC. 12.5% by VOL.
Exclusively for Jason's Vineyard

WINE & FARE

Meritage
Pair with beef, pork, veal, pâté or swordfish.

Chardonnay
Pair with rich seafood and poultry.

Merlot
This wine is a perfect accompaniment to any steak, rib or duck dinner.

Martha Clara Vineyards

Riverhead

Martha Clara Vineyards brings together all of the good things in life: wine, food, families and fun. The motto is "growing magic," and one peek into a vineyard on any given day explains why. Music, laughter, conversation and families fill the winery's venues. Events like Live Mic Night—every Tuesday—and cooking demonstrations are constants on the Martha Clara calendar. The stage has seen Jimmy Buffet, the Supremes' Mary Wilson, the Funk Brothers and Jimmy Cliff perform benefit concerts. Local art, private tastings, film festivals, themed dances, weddings and gourmet wine dinners abound. Children are always welcome and provided with seasonal entertainment; a haunted gingerbread-house decorating workshop is offered in autumn. Even pets are welcome, evidenced by the appearance of Bernie the Jack Russell terrier on his very own line of products—Pinot Poochio. There really is something for everybody.

Providing the public with comfort and taste comes naturally to the founder of Martha Clara Vineyards. It started with the 1995 planting by Robert Entenmann, grandson of William Entenmann, who created the nationally loved line of Entenmann's baked goods. When William Jr. took over his father's retail business on Long Island, he became fond of a young pastry sales girl named Martha Clara Schneider. The two married and continued to nourish the enormously successful company with the help of their three sons. Martha was the support system behind the operation, tirelessly ensuring the quality of the family's products. Her warm presence and business know-how made her an undeniable candidate for Robert's business inspiration. It was clear that Martha Clara Vineyards was the perfect name for his new venture.

Top Left: Heavy medals—from sparkling and aromatic white wines to opulent red and luscious dessert wines, all of the award-winners are 100-percent estate grown.

Bottom Left: The family—Robert Entenmann, Jason Damianos, Jacqueline Entenmann-Damianos and Dr. Dan Damianos—could not be more proud of the winery's success.

Facing Page: Peach trees line a path leading from the vineyards to the main offices. Guests are welcome to pick the fruit, come harvest time.

Situated in Riverhead, on the North Fork of Long Island, the scenic grounds were originally purchased by Robert to raise thoroughbred racehorses. The sprawling countryside is now home to 112 acres of vines, an ambitious number that has jumped from an initial 18 acres of Vitis vinifera. The first release was a well-received 1998 Viognier. Although nearly half of the grapes are merlot—a response to consumer demands—the winery grows a wide array of classic grape varietals like pinot gris, sauvignon blanc, cabernet, cabernet franc and syrah. The team has taken cues from the masters, using familiar viticultural practices to those of their European counterparts. With comparable latitudinal positions, Long Island has a similar climate to Bordeaux, which allows Martha Clara Vineyards to successfully ripen the classic varieties found in the famed region of France. Each year brings out different characteristics in the grapes; Martha Clara's 2000 and 2001 reds have gained special attention for their rich flavors and their line of sparkling wines has garnered high praise from *The New York Times*. Jacqueline Entenmann Damianos, Robert's daughter, and Bob Kern, the general manager, now uphold the winery's standards through daily operations and perpetuate the hospitality that began with Robert's mother. Horses do still appear at Martha Clara, carrying guests through the vineyards on a guided carriage ride. The farm is also home to many rescued animals including alpaca, llamas and Scottish Highland cows, just to name a few.

Top Right: The Culinary Education Center is where international chefs come to show off their talents, set in an intimate loft overlooking the vineyard.

Bottom Right: Warming and inviting, the gallery has an ambience that makes it an ideal space for formal gatherings and casual events alike. *Photograph courtesy of Martha Clara Vineyards*

Facing Page: The tasting room pavilion at Martha Clara Vineyards offers year-round space for wine tastings, picnics, events, wine dinners, and weekly cooking demonstrations.

Top: The thick, green canopy of the B1 block merlot soaks up the sunshine, which helps develop a grape's sugars.

Bottom: Why the long face? Happy and healthy, horses still graze on the farm with Robert Entenmann's house in the background.

Top: Looking west toward the B1 block merlot vines, visitors cannot escape the green countryside.

Bottom: The original fencing from the horse paddock-turned-vineyard remains today.

Through the combination of Old World know-how, modern practices and attention to detail, the integrity of Martha Clara's wines is evident. Juan Micieli-Martinez has brought a strong background to the winery, previously practicing at Pellegrini and Shinn Estate Vineyards. He carries out a medium-density planting strategy that promotes intense fruit flavor. Eager enophiles will get a taste of his first wines with the 2007 vintage. To achieve higher success rates, the winery employed a laser planter, which provided unerringly precise measurements for the vines before the actual sowing. This, plus careful selection of clones and a master winemaker, is a rewarding equation.

Honored on a regional, national and international level, the vineyards have created some of the world's best wine, with regular mentions in *The New York Times*. Included in the lengthy register of awarded wines, the 2000 Merlot and 2002 Ciel, a proprietary blend, both received double gold at the 2004 New York Wine and Food Classic.

Repeatedly generating distinctive dessert wines with numerous gold-status achievements, the Ciel consistently tops the list. The 2006 Tasters Guild International Competition resulted in two gold honors, for the 2004 Gewürztraminer and the 2004 Himmel.

Embracing the community, the vineyard welcomes any cultural event to its home. Urban and developmental pressure on regional wineries has made the founders and staff absolutely committed to the continuation of the Entenmann vision. Not just a company, the winery is a social gathering point, representative of New York and American culture. Always keeping this in mind, the property features the largest art gallery on the east end of Long Island—an impressive 4,000-square-foot space.

Above: The Ark is home to four goats and a one-eared pig named Vincent. Guests are welcome to visit and feed all of the farm animals.

Facing Page: A trifecta: the horse paddock, acres of merlot vines and rows of peach trees line the property.

Supporting local humanities is a priority, offering its stage for poetry readings, comedic acts, independent bands and storytelling. Martha Clara also hosts more than 60 charitable events annually, including animal shelter fundraisers and homeless outreach benefits. A culinary education center features sessions and demonstrations with chef instructors from New York establishments like Buoy One, Jamesport Manor Inn and Q Restaurant. Classes range in size, holding up to 40 students at a time. The winery is constantly looking for new ways to entertain guests and encourage regional sustainability, making it a cultural mecca for Long Island visitors.

Martha Clara
V I N E Y A R D S®
The Entenmann's Family Farm

Wine & Fare

Martha Clara Vineyards Riesling
(100% riesling)
Pair with pad Thai, spicy lobster rolls and red chicken curry.

Martha Clara Vineyards Syrah
(93% syrah, 7% viognier)
Pair with grilled squab with fresh black burgundy truffles and glazed endive; seared calves' liver with caramelized Vidalia onions, applewood smoked bacon and fava beans.

Martha Clara Vineyards 'Five-O' Red Blend
(merlot, cabernet sauvignon, cabernet franc, malbec, petit verdot)
Pair with Bolognese sauce, smoked pork shoulder, parmesan and Cantal cheese.

Martha Clara Vineyards Himmel
(66% riesling, 34% gewürztraminer)
Pair with apple tart with crumbled Roquefort cheese; goat cheese; and almond truffles.

Tastings
Open to the public daily, year-round

Palmer Vineyards

Riverhead

Experience counts: Before selling his advertising firm in Manhattan, Bob Palmer would make weekly visits to his West Coast office in San Francisco. It was here that he developed a taste and fondness for wine. He found himself introducing and explaining vintages and blends at family gatherings and parties, inadvertently playing the role of a wine-tasting guide. Bob soon realized that wine was a daunting subject to the public, inaccessible on many levels. With just a little direction, people became excited to drink and try a variety of wines. Since he had successfully translated the language of wine to his friends and family over time, it seemed only natural for him to do the same on a larger scale.

Determined to make good wine more readily approachable to the populace, Bob has used his marketing know-how to do just that by starting Palmer Vineyards. He planted the winery's first vines in 1983 and opened for business two years later on the north fork of Long Island. The winery consists of two main vineyards totaling over 120 acres, the second one supplying the lion's share of the whites.

A twist of bad luck brought Hurricane Gloria raging into the Eastern Seaboard in September of 1985, causing the vineyard's first vintage to take a serious blow. Hard work and determination, however, kept the winery afloat. Despite the original setback, Palmer Vineyards would grow to become what *The New York Times* wine critic Howard Goldberg called "Long Island's most important winery."

Top & Bottom Left: A healthy vineyard is key to achieving gold medal-winning wines.

Facing Page: The gently rolling hillsides counterbalance the sometimes-harsh weather.

The plantings began as a series of guesswork. Unsure of what would react well to the region, Bob and his team planted several varietals including merlot, chardonnay, zinfandel and pinot blanc. Because it had a short growing season compared to other grapes, merlot quickly became the vineyard's mainstay. At that time, it had not reached the widespread popularity that it has found today and was a signature of the vineyards. Zinfandel was quickly ruled out as a feasible crop while non-chardonnay whites became some of the best in the nation. Rieslings and sauvignon blancs have been consistently applauded. Medaling in the 2005 Finger Lakes International Competition, the white riesling proves itself as a classic summer wine, exhibiting floral and fruit accents with lightly sweet spiciness. The 2006 Sauvignon Blanc was grown at the vineyard in Peconic—the second, aforementioned site—where the wine was fermented in stainless steel tanks to ensure the prevalence of the fruit's pure flavors. Dominant citrus and green apple notes come out of this straw-colored vintage, with undertones of mineral and lemon peel.

Right: Both French and American oak barrels are used at Palmer.

Facing Page: Palmer's property encompasses nearly 200 acres and is divided into two main vineyards.

COOPERAGE

The Ancient Greeks learned that if wine is allowed to "breathe" small amounts of air a magical improvement occurs in certain wine during what is called the aging p The first aging was done in earthenware crocks. In the middle ages French and wine makers began using oak cooperage which allows the wine to breathe and its' own pleasant flavor.
These oak casks were purchased in France. French oak is considered the best f Here we age our Chardonnay, Merlot and Cabernet.
The time spent in the cask varies between 8 weeks and 18 months, depending grape and the wine maker.
Incidentally, after 5-7 years the casks no longer impart their special flavor and replaced.

Bringing the grapes to life, winemaker Miguel Martin arrived with a world of experience. With a resume that reads like a travelogue, he has worked in Toledo, Spain, as a technical director, as well as California, Chile and Australia. New York wineries rely heavily on the knowledge and skill of a winemaker due to the Northeast's harsh weather. Miguel's talents, then, are of the utmost importance to the vineyard's products. Helping to make up for a severe climate, the relatively flat, slightly rolling hills help provide an ideal grape-growing environment. This regional topography allows for minimal water run-off, aiding in simpler irrigational management.

Many American states—from coast to coast—carry the Palmer title. Upholding his love of advertising, Bob spends about half of the year traveling to spread the word of wine. His supportive family helps make this possible, as they do a great deal of work for daily operations. Two of his three daughters help with the corporate side of the production: Kathy works as the business manager and Barbara, a lawyer, handles all legalities that go along with owning a business. His wife, Lorraine, and middle daughter, Lori, design custom gift baskets, adding a personally

crafted touch. This strong foundation coupled with Bob's aggressive marketing efforts have resulted in the vineyard receiving widespread recognition, making it a well-known winery name on Long Island.

Events that appeal to the whole family help to give Palmer Vineyards its distinctiveness. During the fall, guests come from near and far to enjoy the Harvest Festival Hayride Hoedown—full of bluegrass and country music. The spectacular vineyard is toured while riders sip on the land's bounty, offering a cup of crowd-pleasing Kool-Aid to the children. With a laid-back, easy feel, the vineyards invite all walks of life to come, drink and just have a good time. For more romantic affairs, a cruise company features gourmet food and lets Palmer wines flow while traveling up the Hudson River Valley.

Above: Guests are invited to take a self-guided tour to learn about the winery as well as Long Island's rich heritage of winemaking.

Facing Page Top: Arguably the best part of the tour is the final stop: the tasting room.

Facing Page Bottom: The 19th-century English pub-style tasting room provides a great ambience for sampling fine wine.

With fun promotions that have an all-encompassing appeal, it is no wonder that Palmer Vineyards has achieved a wide market. Over time, the establishment has served as the official winery of the New York Yankees and Mets radio networks, and functioned as a key sponsor for the Brooklyn Cyclones and Long Island Ducks baseball teams. In honor of the game, fans had the opportunity to show their baseball caps in exchange for a price reduction on bottles of wine. Purposely broadening the scope of people's wine-friendly food associations, Palmer Vineyards offered free hotdogs with the purchase of a glass of wine on summer holiday weekends. Good wine should not be limited to high-end food.

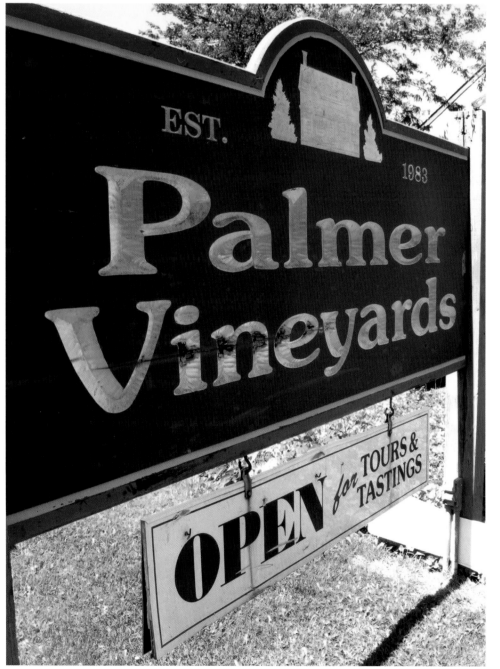

Top & Bottom Left: Palmer Vineyards' tasting house overlooks 65 acres of lush vineyards and boasts the most beautiful sunset views on the North Fork.
Photographs by Bridget Quinn Micieli-Martinez

Facing Page: Guests can relax with a glass of wine while gazing upon the verdant, rolling vineyards.
Photograph by Amanda DeAnglis

As president of the Long Island Wine Council, Bob keeps his finger on the pulse of the industry. Founded in 1989, the group aims to develop the local trade and bring recognition to what the area can offer the wine world. Bob knows that the majority of vineyard visitors come from the same small percentage of the population, usually wine enthusiasts who travel from region to region. With proper promotion and the help of organizations like the wine council, the remainder of the population will become interested in what wineries have to offer. Long Island has such a wide array of high-quality wines to offer; even the simplest palate can find a favorite.

WINE & FARE

Chardonnay Reserve

Pair with a variety of foods, such as grilled salmon or pasta with a cream sauce.

Sauvignon Blanc

Pair with appetizers, salads, grilled chicken or fish, and many spicy ethnic dishes.

Merlot

Delicious with many foods, such as roast chicken or grilled flank steak.

Cabernet Franc

Pair with pork dishes, baked fruit, a variety of red meat, or simply serve by itself.

Tastings
Open to the public daily, year-round

Peconic Bay Winery

Cutchogue

A breezy knoll more than 100 feet above the magnificent Long Island Sound affords views across the sparkling white caps, as well as warmth from the summer sun. The muted calls of the swooping seabirds momentarily distract from the endless view of the Connecticut and Rhode Island shorelines, and a snap of the sea air provides refreshment.

Turning around, the eyes grasp for reference points as they sweep over thousands of acres of ancient farmlands, for which the North Fork of Long Island has been famed. Directly ahead, rolling away in perfectly ordered rows are 35 acres of some of the finest vinifera vineyards in America. This is the breathtaking Oregon Hills property, 147 acres in total, of Peconic Bay Winery, owned by Ursula and Paul Lowerre and their family.

While driving down the mile-long road through the vineyards, the owners feel less a part of reality and more like they have gone on vacation. It is hard for them to imagine that they actually own something so profoundly beautiful—the majestic landscape is so moving, they almost forget its immense responsibilities.

It all began when the Manhattan couple was looking to buy some land as a passive investment; they never dreamed the search would ultimately lead to the ownership of an important winery. In 1997 Paul and Ursula acquired their winery's land overlooking Long Island Sound, much of it planted with grains and potatoes. Now, 35 of those acres produce excellent merlot and chardonnay fruit—the beginning of many grapes to come. The 1999 purchase of an existing winery with 24 acres of mature vines put the Lowerre family in the wine business in a big way. They have since added cabernet sauvignon,

Top Left: Wine tastings let visitors scope out their favorite vintage.
Photograph courtesy of Mitre Agency

Bottom Left: A big sign on the main road in Cutchogue, directs wine enthusiasts to their destination.
Photograph courtesy of Mitre Agency

Facing Page: Some of the oldest vines in Long Island make Peconic Bay wines.
Photograph courtesy of Mitre Agency

cabernet franc, riesling, plus Bordeaux blends to their portfolio. Winery whites have pulled in wide recognition; the La Barrique Chardonnay has three Best of New York State awards under its belt, and the Riesling was recently named Top Ten—United States in an important international tasting in Australia. Polaris, the signature riesling dessert wine, offers the perfect finish to an evening meal. So perfect in fact, that Alex von Bidder, an owner of New York City's fabled Four Seasons Restaurant once said it reminded him of his home in Austria.

Ursula and Paul are no strangers to wine; they have grown up with it. All of their parents were wine lovers, in a time when many folks simply nursed a Scotch all through dinner. Ursula's father preferred Bordeaux, while Paul's father kept Beaune reds in his cellar. This gave them both a familiarity and a disarming ease with wine, which carries over to the guiding philosophy at Peconic Bay Winery. For them, wine has never been an intimidating mystery or a point of pretension; wine is simply an integral part of the four Fs—food, family, friends and fun. As a result, Peconic Bay wines are crafted, above all else, to enhance any gathering where food is involved, especially the fresh produce harvested locally. Their house style is about bright varietal flavors and a structure that refreshes the palate. Forget about winning cult wine competitions; Peconic Bay Winery wants to shine at the dinner table—or even the picnic table.

Top Right: Pressing the grapes reveals the rich colors of the fruit.

Bottom Right: Barreling the wine is a critical stage in developing the wines' flavors.
Photograph courtesy of Mitre Agency

Facing Page: The tasting room includes a beautiful mural of the vineyard.

Ursula and Paul have raised their daughters, Lavinia and Cornelia, into the same wine customs and traditions as they enjoyed, and both are taking active roles in shaping Peconic Bay's future. Lavinia, whose wine of choice is the Steel-Fermented Chardonnay, is bringing her experience and academic background to the winery's marketing activities. She is hard at work developing the brand image and all aspects of the client experience; when guests visit the winery in the summer and fall, they will feel her creative energy in all the events and activities in and around the gorgeous tasting room. Cornelia is involved with promoting Peconic Bay Winery in Upstate New York, which is her home for now—cabernet franc is her favorite wine.

Peconic Bay Winery owes much of its success to the careful assembling of an amazing team of vintners and vineyardists, all indigenous to the North Fork. Here again, Ursula and Paul want Peconic Bay Winery to reflect the very best of the soil and climate of the North Fork, and who better to coax that out than agriculturalists who have committed much of their lives to tending vines and making wine in this region.

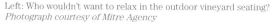

Left: Who wouldn't want to relax in the outdoor vineyard seating?
Photograph courtesy of Mitre Agency

Facing Page: Simple charm reigns in the tasting room.

Matthew Gillies has been a key player in the Lowerres' journey, first helping them assemble the properties, later organizing the winery's acquisition, and now serving as the general manager of the entire project. As a budding vineyardist in the '70s, he was a member of the pioneering Hargrave Vineyards team. Greg Gove, Peconic Bay's affable and expert winemaker, mixes his chemistry background with more than two decades of vinification experience to produce consistently palate-pleasing wines. He came into the industry as cellar master for Hargrave Vineyards in 1985, a time when the Long Island wine region was still a small town. Charlie Hargrave—sporting an obvious connection to the founding family of Long Island wine—serves as the vineyard manager. Vine after vine, row after row, the plants are immaculately trimmed, giving the area one of its most memorable views. Ursula and Paul look forward to years of great winemaking, and the great fun of working with such dedicated and expert professionals.

Of all the benefits—and problems—that come with owning a winery, the Lowerres put one above the rest: the preservation of land. They are a part of the amazing open vistas along Oregon Road with many hundreds of acres of agricultural land. They know that if wineries, vineyards and farms did not occupy the North Fork land, commercial and residential development might take over one of the most beautiful regions in the United States. Furthering their community's preservation and protection, the couple supports the Peconic Land Trust, the Wildlife Trust's Peconic Bay Sea Turtle Project, Cornell University's College of Agriculture and Life Sciences, and New York City's Central Park Conservancy, among others.

Above Left: Alfresco seating is perfect for all types of gatherings.
Photograph courtesy of Mitre Agency

Above Right: Table settings on the covered terrace accommodate any number of occasions.
Photograph courtesy of Mitre Agency

Facing Page: Sunny days lend themselves to ideal settings for sipping wine.
Photograph courtesy of Mitre Agency

The Lowerres love to gather some friends at the winery in Cutchogue, fire up the grills, get some music going, pull some corks and glory in the beauty of the sunniest town in New York State. They graciously invite all to bring some friends and family to their winery, pick up a bottle of wine, pull up some Adirondack chairs and enjoy the setting. If it is possible to bottle warmth, fun and generosity of spirit, the Lowerre family and Peconic Bay Winery have done it on the North Fork of Long Island.

PECONIC BAY
WINERY

WINE & FARE

La Barrique Chardonnay
(100% chardonnay)

Pair with grilled chicken; rich seafood; creamy sauces that include apple, lemon, garlic, dill, basil and ginger.

Riesling
(100% riesling)

Pair with shellfish; white fish such as bass or trout; and it brings a wonderful cooling touch to spicy Asian cuisine.

Cabernet Franc
(75% cabernet franc, 20% cabernet sauvignon, 5% merlot)

Pair with duck in a raspberry reduction; beef fillets in a mushroom demi-glace; or just about anything off the grill.

Tastings
Open to the public daily, year-round

Pindar Vineyards

Peconic

The history of Pindar Vineyards begins around 520 BC when one of the greatest Western poets was born just outside of Thebes. His subsequent life of traveling, writing, and reciting Hellenic verses made him a canon in the Greek culture and proved enough to inspire Herodotus Damianos to name his youngest child in honor of Pindar. And even though Peconic's Pindar Vineyards opened when Pindar, the boy, was too young to drink wine, he now runs the winery, overseeing operations of 600 acres as vineyard manager. Pindar's education included an associate's degree at Cobleskill in agronomy studies and a bachelor's degree in enology and viticulture from the University of California at Fresno, along with the virtue of living in a family of vintners. Growing grapes that include chardonnay, cabernet franc, malbec, riesling, gamay and viognier, the winery produces enough varieties for any palate. Embracing tradition, the Damianos' approach steers clear of pesticides in order to uphold earth-friendly methods and maintain superior grape flavors. But there is nothing surprising about the use of classic techniques in this family—the Long Island industry they have built thrives on old European traditions and the ideals of classic Greek civilization.

Top Left: Pindar Damianos is right at home in the barrel room.

Bottom Left: The tasting room offers visitors Chardonnay Reserve, Mythology, Johannesburg Riesling, Cabernet Sauvignon and Syrah, among others.

Facing Page: A view of the vineyards in the fall keeps people returning year after year.
Photograph by Ralph Pugliese, Jr.

Growing grapes in Mattituck, Cutchogue, Peconic and Southold, the Damianos family has taken advantage of the Bordeaux-like climate in the region. Temperatures stay in check with the help of surrounding water, the Atlantic Ocean offers its elements to both areas. Over time, the climates produce grapes that give wine a lower alcohol content, offering the drinker elegance that is worthy of a food companion. Wines like Pythagoras—a non-vintage blend of cabernet sauvignon, cabernet franc, petit verdot, malbec and merlot—and the complex Mythology really show the flavor of Long Island. Pythagoras won the distinction as Best US Red Blend by the Chicago Tasting Institute and Best Red Vinifera during the Best of the East Competition. Commissioning a local artist to create the perfect images, the family shows pride in their past, featuring names that pay homage to Mediterranean roots. Inspiring images of Jason's ship, The Good Ship Argo, appear on the merlot, while mosaics of Dionysus riding a vineyard-hopping leopard on the chardonnay reserve and representations of Pegasus appear on the cabernet sauvignon.

Top & Bottom Right: A tasting room should always greet visitors with relaxed surroundings, friendly staff and plenty of wine.

Facing Page: The front façade of Pindar Vineyards welcomes guests from across the country.

Top: Events and gatherings come alive on the pavilion.

Middle & Bottom: Each harvest season the harvester is put to work, gathering grapes for the wine.

Left: The vineyard speaks for itself—it is absolutely beautiful.

So how did the legend of Pindar Vineyards begin? What inspired Herodotus, or Dr. Dan as he is affectionately called, came as he began his life as a practicing internist in 1966. Taking on a home that had previously sat empty for about 30 years, Dr. Dan and his wife undertook a great deal of sprucing up. Little did he know the most rewarding spruce-up would be in the forgotten grape arbors just outside the home. Sensitive to nature and the blessings it bestows, Mrs. Damianos, Dr. Dan's mother, introduced a strong connection to the outdoors. So, he took note of the Niagara vines that twisted and turned through the moist dirt, not demanding Dr. Dan's attention until the warmth of summer brought fruit. The timing could not have been more perfect. A

seeming misfortune, the nematode had infected area potato crops and prevented the growth and harvest of a staple; potatoes had to take a hiatus. In the interim however, the land opened up for nematode-proof crops: Vitis vinifera. Once Dr. Dan began planting, history was made and Long Island's world of wine commenced.

Above: Whether standing inside the vineyards' rows or on the pavilion just beyond, the view is impressive.
Photograph by Ralph Pugliese, Jr.

Facing Page: The tasting bar serves thousands of visitors each year.

Reaching the pinnacle of entrepreneurial success, Dr. Dan and his sons sell approximately 60,000 cases of wine per year in a variety of intensities and prices, ensuring nearly every wine drinker has an option. Wineries have sprung up across the North Fork, affirming his sound business decisions from decades earlier. But perhaps the most flattering of all accomplishments in Dr. Dan's long road as a vintner came in 1989. President George H.W. Bush served Pindar selections at his inaugural dinner, the 1986 Chardonnay and the 1986 Cabernet Sauvigon. Phone calls and press flooded the winery, sales soared and Dr. Dan knew that he had not only chosen the right direction in his career, he had reached the top.

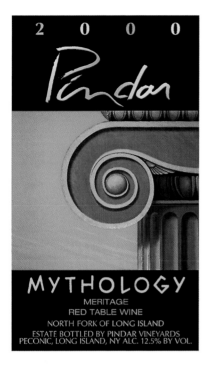

WINE & FARE

Chardonnay Dessert Wine
Pair with pumpkin spice mousse, apricot honey tart or rustic pear cake drizzled with cardamom and anise syrup.

Mythology
Try this wine with linguine, squid and scallops in a roasted tomato sauce or roasted pork tenderloin in a tangy red currant sauce.

Johannesburg Riesling
Pair with roast quail and autumn-fruit stuffing, baked trout in almond-basil pesto or phyllo-wrapped brie with an apricot, pecan and sage chutney.

Tastings
Open to the public daily, year-round

 # Raphael

Peconic

The slow food movement has forced societies to pause and embrace the gifts of cuisine; Raphael on Long Island has adapted a similar approach to its vineyards: slow wine. Here, wine is not hurried. Wine is grown, not made. Every step in the winemaking process has an appreciative value to it. The staff at Raphael holds this philosophy close, keeping a keen eye on the vines at all times without interfering in the flavor development of the natural cycle.

Raphael lies just 90 miles east of Manhattan—but the pace makes it feel like it is a world away. Led by winemaker Richard Olsen-Harbich, the production process holds true to traditional standards, drawing on all elements related to the wine: food, agriculture, romance, creativity. Just as winemakers long ago, Raphael harvests all of the grapes on its estate by hand and utilizes a wooden basket press, the only East Coast winery to do so for commercial use. Gentle and pressure free, this step extracts all the desirable elements from the grapes, leaving behind the bitter, less tasty components often found in mass-produced wines. The process is especially beneficial to reds, making merlot the most prized and perfected wine of Raphael, with approximately half of its acreage devoted to the grape. The downfalls of artisanal crafting in the wine industry are certainly present; the wooden basket press is cumbersome, difficult to clean and only handles relatively small quantities. "It's worth it," says Richard, as it allows wine drinkers to taste the flavor of hand-picking and the classic trade.

Top Left: Raphael's First Label Merlot and Sauvignon Blanc are signature wines.

Bottom Left: Merlot clusters cling to the vine, ripening to their peak just before harvest.

Facing Page: The magnificent Raphael winery structure is as much of a draw for visitors as the wine.

This love of traditionalism began with Raphael Petrocelli, a man with Italian roots. Raphael shared his interest in winemaking with his son John, unknowingly starting a lifelong passion for the art. A devotion to his family guided John to establish Raphael Vineyards—with a clear tribute to his father—in 1996 on a 60-acre site in the hamlet of Peconic.

The timing was ideal; Long Island had grown to understand its region and see the viticultural potential by the mid-'90s. Climatological studies in the late '80s revealed information about the North Fork's ideal terroir, where previously California had been the only place in the United States to receive such attention. The Bordeaux-like setting promises a maritime climate with four distinct seasons and glacially deposited soil for thriving European varietals. Knowing this plus having a team of vintners with state-of-the-art expertise forced the company to take a close look at its direction. Awareness, consistency and quality take top-ranking priorities. With the counsel of consulting enologist Paul Pontallier of the famed Château Margaux, the company has made a concerted effort to bring the world a handful of beautifully executed wines without the distraction of too many products. Time, energy and focus go into what matters: the wine.

Top Right: The entrance to the Raphael cellar welcomes guests with warm earth tones and barrels of wine.

Middle Right: Raphael's temperature-controlled fermentation tanks comprise one step in the winemaking process.

Bottom Right: Nestled inside the barrel cave, Raphael's wine library holds some of the state's most savored vintages.

Facing Page: The visitor center uses Old World architecture and rich woods to capture the spirit of the winery.

Reflecting the Petrocelli heritage, John has fashioned Raphael after a Mediterranean villa, romantic and warm. This carries over to the events held within its walls, including weddings, corporate events and family gatherings. Surrounded in elegance and adventure, the aptly named Renaissance Room can hold nearly 200 guests, showing off antique finishes with polished cherry and deep mahogany detailing.

Under the watch of the 35-year veteran vineyard manager Steven Mudd, sustainable agricultural practices have resulted in a pure expression of terroir. Now a dying breed in other parts of the world, meticulous hand work is used by the Raphael staff on its three main varieties: the aforementioned merlot, sauvignon blanc and cabernet franc as well as on the smaller plantings of cabernet sauvignon, malbec and petit verdot. Steven's longtime Long Island experience informs his techniques; from pruning and leaf-pulling to picking, the staff enforces

close quality control at every step. With no short-cuts, additives or harmful chemicals, the sustainable initiatives have resulted in a sincere, straightforward wine.

Above Left: Awaiting their flavorful fate, hand-picked merlot grapes await processing on the crush deck.

Above Right: Small baskets are used to take the harvest from the vineyard, the most efficient and manageable means of transporting the fruit.

Facing Page: Raphael's sauvignon blanc vineyard is home to both mature and young vines.

Numerous mentions from *The New York Times* wine critic Howard Goldberg have affirmed that the detailed, classic approach to vinification is working and that Raphael's First Label Merlot is, in fact, top-notch. Critics and connoisseurs will agree: This is a winery not to be missed.

WINE & FARE

Sauvignon Blanc
(100% sauvignon blanc)

Pair with broiled striped bass, oysters, shrimp scampi and vegetarian cuisine.

First Label Merlot
(95% merlot, 5% malbec)

Pair with rack of lamb, roast Long Island duck, aged prime rib, and blue-vein cheeses.

Cabernet Franc
(100% cabernet franc)

Pair with aged goat cheese, veal, grilled tuna and roast loin of pork.

Steel-Fermented Chardonnay
(100% chardonnay)

Pair with crab cakes, grilled chicken Niçoise salad, and mild cheeses.

Tastings
Open to the public daily, by appointment

Sherwood House Vineyards

Mattituck

F rancophiles, world-travelers and connoisseurs—Charles and Barbara Smithen have all the qualities that make great vintners.

Interest in wine began years ago for Charles, as he studied medicine in London. Delighted by the unexpected viticulture, Charles was welcomed to the dinner tables of his British friends. Much like the French do while dining out, the English had elaborate meals with wine at every course. Aperitifs, whites, reds, dessert wines and ports stretched through meals, giving young Charles' palate a flavorful lesson.

Never forgetting his days under the English influence, Charles and his wife Barbara spent a great deal of time tasting their way through France—Burgundy, Avignon, Loire Valley, Provence. Reflecting these journeys and flavors, the Smithens opened the boutique-type Sherwood House Vineyards on the North Fork of Long Island in Mattituck. More like a hidden treasure tucked in the French countryside than a Long Island New York winery, the 38-and-a-half-acre spread has a renovated farmhouse from 1860 and was once home to rows and rows of corn and potato crops. Taking cue from its French influence, Sherwood House Vineyards' tasting room is an unassuming cottage, packed full of hospitality. But make no mistake about it—this tiny tasting room leaves a powerful impression, winning North Fork's Best Tasting Room award in 2007. Barbara runs the cottage and makes everyone who enters feel right at home. Often, the Smithens can be found signing bottles, laughing with guests and telling stories about their corkscrew collection. No doubt, these personal touches keep visitors coming back.

Top Left: Nearly used as the company label, a 1933 Leonetto Cappiello poster from the French wine council reads, *Buvez du vin et vivez joyeux,* or drink wine and live joyously. The phrase appears on every Sherwood label.

Bottom Left: Among the many antiques owned by Barbara and Charles, this turn-of-the-century wooden cart sits on the property—once used to asphalt the winery's main road.

Facing Page: A 1953 Studebaker pick-up truck reveals the personality and appeal of the winery.

1996 saw the successful five-acre planting of Dijon-cloned chardonnay grapes at Sherwood House Vineyards. Since Burgundy is home to the finest chardonnays in the world—Dijon is the culturally rich capital of the Burgundy province—the wine results have been second-to-none. With less oak-flavor than their California counterparts, Burgundian chardonnays have thrived in Long Island's climate, bringing the vineyards numerous awards including a win at the London International Wine and Spirits competition. In the following years, cabernet sauvignon, merlot, petit verdot and cabernet franc have also fared well under Sherwood's care, offering near-perfect grapes during the hand-picked harvest.

As the years go by, Sherwood House Vineyards is racking up its awards, including honors from the New York Food and Wine Classic; the Los Angeles International Competition; and a near-clean sweep with 11 of 12 medals at the Miami International Fair.

So, who are the artists behind the label? For one, winemaker Gilles Martin. Born in Meaux, France, and obtaining a master's degree in enology at the esteemed Université Montepellier I, Gilles adds traditional craftsmanship and decades of practice to the team. His portfolio includes a years-long stint at Delas-Freres in the Rhône Valley and work with the production of some of the world's most well-known wines—Hermitage and Chateauneuf du Pape. Add in his time in Mendocino County, California, and the results show fine-tuned skill with an unmatchable palate.

Above: Whether in the Loire Valley or the North Fork, the sight of thriving grapes under the morning sun can captivate any wine lover.

Right: Chardonnay grapes were the first planted on the vineyards, cloned from Burgundy-style vines. Merlot, cabernet franc, petit verdot and cabernet sauvignon were soon to follow.

Facing Page Top: Seventeenth- and 18th-century English drinking glasses with rare spiral stems sit with 19th-century Bristol glasses—an exceptional collection. The toastmaster glass is included, made entirely of thick-glass interior that allows one ounce of wine for a toast.

Facing Page Bottom: The original Sherwood label rendering by Michael Croteau hangs above a collection of bas armanacs, ranging from 1904 through the rare 1942—Charles' year of birth.

Vineyard manager and expert Steven Mudd has been with the Smithens since the beginning. Work with his father in a self-started vineyard consulting company has added volumes of knowledge to the management and developing of the prosperous boutique vineyards. Upstarts in the New York wine industry, Steven and his father began the second vinifera vineyard on Long Island. He is as much a part of the land as the vines he devotedly grows—acknowledged with his two-time achievement as Grower of the Year.

With a constant eye on the horizon, Sherwood House Vineyards is perpetually looking to bring high quality wine to those who love it. An exciting Bordeaux blend and a rosé—combining a perfect mixture of merlot and syrah—are sure to please Sherwood fans. Quantities will remain limited, as only the finest fruit is used in production.

Top Left: The Old World cart stands as an indicator of time gone by. Once used for corn and potato crops, the land exhibited ideal conditions for grape growing.

Middle Left: An array of rare-patent antique corkscrews consists of 19th-century English models—perfect complements to an Old World winery. One of only three in the world, a Tom Cotterill patent appears in both the Smithens' collection and on the back of every wine bottle.

Bottom Left: Circa 1880, antique pipes include meerschaum, carved in Paris and Vienna, and Napoleon on the left.

Facing Page: The vineyards seem to say the same printed adage on the back of every wine bottle: *Buvez du vin et vivez joyeux.*

French wines are not only in France, thanks to the Smithens. Warm and humble to its European roots, Sherwood House Vineyards epitomizes good taste and charm.

WINE & FARE

Sherwood Manor Blend

Pair with daube de boeuf Provencal—a rich, French beef stew filled with vegetables and herbs.

Sherwood House Vineyards Chardonnay

Pair with angel hair pasta and a light pesto sauce, preferably made with a fruity Greek olive oil, hazelnuts, plenty of fresh basil and a hint of lemon.

Merlot

Pairs easily with a wide variety of entrées and side dishes— rosemary chicken; Indian-spiced meats; potato dishes; vanilla or fruit-scented sauces.

Tastings

Open to the public Friday through Sunday, seasonally

Wölffer Estate Vineyard

Sagaponack

A leader in sustainable farming and Long Island winemaking, Wölffer Estate Vineyard is idyllically nestled between Southampton and East Hampton, just 2.6 miles from the Atlantic. The unique terroir, similar in many respects to that of Bordeaux, allows Wölffer Estate to produce award-winning wines with a rich concentration of fruit and lively acidity. Though the winery boasts a state-of-the-art winemaking facility—complete with computerized stainless-steel tanks, laboratory, bottling line and cellar—Wölffer maintains a decidedly European character and an organic, Old World-style grape-growing philosophy.

Hand-picking and manually sorting 60 acres of grapes is certainly not the simplest start to creating wine, but for Wölffer's passionate proprietor, winemaker, vineyard manager and staff members it is the only option. A perfection-based process yields perfection in every bottle. Everyone at Wölffer Estate acts as a steward of the land and wholly embraces the organization's eco-conscious, non-interventionist approach to agriculture. A drip irrigation system—used sparingly—nourishes the vines when rainfall is low and extends the time frame for growing and ripening. Wölffer Estate is one of few vineyards that has never had mechanical harvesting or leaf-removal equipment. Machines simply cannot be expected to make the important decisions that workers do as they progress through row after row of flourishing fruit. Picked late in the season for peak sugar levels, grapes move from vine to crush pad to refrigerated tank in less than two hours, ensuring that every ounce of flavor and freshness is preserved. Although the Wölffer staff clearly has the art of grape growing down to a science, such impeccable logistics continue to be fine tuned each year, demonstrating commitment to excellence and dedication to a slow and gentle approach that produces individually styled wines.

Top Left: Christian Wölffer, owner of Wölffer Estate Vineyard, planted the first vines in 1987.
Photograph courtesy of Wölffer Estate Vineyard

Bottom Left: Two of Wölffer Estate's handcrafted wines wait for visitors to arrive.
Photograph courtesy of Wölffer Estate Vineyard

Facing Page: Merlot vines flourish at the crest of the vineyard. The winery practices sustainable agriculture and is committed to a detailed, hands-on approach that results in a full expression of the unique Sagaponack terroir.

Many people are hard pressed to believe that what is now a multimillion-dollar, internationally renowned operation was born a relatively short time ago, in 1988, when German-born business magnate Christian Wölffer acquired a 14-acre parcel of potato farmland in the heart of the Hamptons to build a home and small horse barn for his young family. The private barn has since expanded to an 80-stall equestrian center. Wölffer Estate Stables, home to Christian's cherished Warmblood horses, has the largest indoor riding arena on the East Coast and is used for schooling, breeding, year-round boarding and instruction. An avid equestrian and consummate entrepreneur involved in a variety of business arenas—investment banking, venture capital, real estate and agriculture, among others—Christian decided to follow his father's dream of being a vineyard and winery owner, expanding his fluency in six languages to a seventh: winemaking. While few understood Christian's vision when he planted the first vines in 1987, his winery's annual production and international distribution of 20,000 cases confirm his decision.

In 1992 Christian brought on German-born winemaker Roman Roth, whose father was a winemaker and barrel maker, and native Long Islander Richard Pisacano as vineyard manager a few years later. Both gentlemen

Top Left: The elegant boutique in the tasting room of the estate offers wine-inspired items and gifts.

Bottom Left: Wölffer Estate Brut Blanc de Blanc and Noblesse Oblige Sparkling Rosé slowly mature in the dimly lit underground cuvee room. Classic sparkling wines are made in the traditional méthode Champenoise.

Facing Page Top: The high-ceilinged Tuscan-style tasting room shows off 100-year-old rough-hewn beams and solid terracotta floors. Guests have the opportunity to sample award-winning wines, take a tour of the winery, cellar and vineyards, or just relax on the terrace overlooking the seemingly endless rows of vines.

Facing Page Bottom: In the European tradition, the barrel rooms are constructed of high-vaulted caves. Wines are aged in imported French oak barrels. A bride and groom sneak a kiss under the watchful eye of Bacchus.
Photograph by Timothy K. Lee

began their careers in the wine industry in their teenage years. At the tender age of 16, Roman began a three-year apprenticeship at a winery in Oberrotweil, Germany, and then traveled the world with extended stays in Carneros, California; New South Wales, Australia; and Baden, Germany, before establishing permanent residence in New York. He brought to the promising upstart winery a master's degree in winemaking and a wealth of practical experience. Roman's counterpoint in the field, Richard, began his career while still in high school, learning to install, control and manage the growth of grapevines at his first winery. The second vineyard refined his knowledge of grafting grapes to produce higher quality fruit and improved yields. His skills have been tested at Wölffer Estate and at his own 11-acre vineyard and limited-production winery on the North Fork of Long Island. Roman, Richard and Christian have been collaborating since the birth of the winery to maximize the full potential of the land and all that it produces. The vineyard and winery are not separate entities that merely make the best of what they're given. Their directors are in constant communication to improve the

process each year—coordinating the timing and logistics of picking, separating small vineyard lots for special treatment, and responding to the changes from vintage to vintage.

Wölffer Estate Vineyard wines fully embody The Hamptons appellation. The ripe fruit of ideal acidity and sugar levels is created from a desirable blend of geographic circumstances—Bridgehampton loam soil, a byproduct of the glacial debris that is marked by sand, silt and clay; a climate that invites refreshing breezes from the nearby Atlantic, cool nights and an extended growing season. The soil type and depth combined with the moderate climate encourage slow and

Above: Wölffer's beautiful and impressive terrace overlooking the vineyard is the perfect venue for the ultimate vineyard wedding, private party or corporate event. During the summer, Wölffer Estate Vineyard is a social mecca with a busy calendar of events. Throughout the year, Twilight Thursdays offer live jazz, complimentary cheese and wine sold by the glass.
Photograph by Timothy K. Lee

Right: Roman Roth has served as the estate's winemaker since 1992.
Photograph courtesy of Wölffer Estate Vineyard

Facing Page Bottom: The hydrangea-bordered gazebo surrounded by merlot vines is a favorite area for wedding ceremonies and secret proposals.

steady ripening, allowing the Wölffer team to harvest late in the year. Wölffer Estate's wines cover the complete spectrum of fine elixirs. Each one is unique, yet all marry classical European style with regional authenticity. All are made for longevity, with a depth and elegance that improves with age. All are created with gastronomy in mind, intended to complement a healthy variety of cuisines.

In the Tuscan-style tasting room, guests are invited to sample a range of wine flights and artisanal cheeses via table service or casually at the bar. French doors open onto a flower-lined stone terrace that affords one of the wine country's most picturesque vineyard views. The beautiful winery is a popular venue for private parties, weddings and corporate events. Below the tasting room is the winemaking facility. In keeping with the European tradition, it includes a wine library, as well as barrel rooms constructed of high-vaulted caves. Wines are aged in French oak barriques to allow the fruitful essences to come through. The wines'

ripe flavors express the way the fruit grows in the vineyard. Richard is ever-experimenting with improved trellising systems, creative irrigation layouts and sustainable farming. He and the rest of the Wölffer team are extremely eco-minded and actively participate in the Long Island sustainable Viticulture Program, which encourages stewardship of the land.

Demonstrating the authentically handmade quality of Wölffer's wines, the winemaker himself often leads tours of the estate. His enthusiasm for the art and craft is evident in every sip of his creations. It is also evident in the fact that he sometimes breaks into song while down in the cellar or barrel room. Guests love it!

Above: Meticulously manicured chardonnay vines welcome visitors. The architecture of the winery is Tuscan in style, with exterior walls of sun-bleached ocher and windows framed in shutters of vibrant Provencal blue.
Photograph by Walter Kober

Facing Page: Lush and green, the estate vineyards reveal the Hamptons' countryside attraction.

The 12,000-square-foot Old World-style winery is set on a hill for panoramic views of the vineyards to the east and the rolling landscape of The Hamptons to the west. Whether guests are relaxing with a glass of Wölffer's legendary wine, touring the vineyards and winery, or attending a wedding or live music event, the delights of Wölffer are endless. Indeed, Wölffer Estate Vineyard is truly an American winery in the classic European tradition.

WÖLFFER ESTATE
VINEYARD

WINE & FARE

Rosé
Pairs well with practically any food. Smoked salmon, shellfish and Thanksgiving turkey are especially good matches.

Caya Cabernet Franc
A great table wine, this rich red, aromatic wine pairs with any red meat, poultry or veal.

Perle Chardonnay
This classic Burgundian-style chardonnay pairs perfectly with rich fish dishes, chicken, veal or an array of cheeses.

Late Harvest Chardonnay
Serve chilled with desserts; also recommended to match with the classic pairing of foie gras or chocolate truffles.

Tastings
Open to the public, year-round

Photograph courtesy of Clark CSM Marketing Communications

Millbrook Vineyards & Winery, *page 116*

Hudson Valley

Benmarl Winery

Marlboro

Imagine loving a job so much, that living at work would be a privilege. Benmarl Winery lies amongst steep-terraced vineyards in the green, rolling Hudson River region—a scene that would stop any wine lover or naturalist dead in his tracks. As proprietor of Benmarl Winery, Victor Spaccarelli Jr. wakes up for work each day in this setting, on the land that he and his family claim is nothing short of magical.

Shrouded in historical significance with an undeniable charm, Benmarl Winery is America's oldest continuously growing vineyard. French Huguenots first saw the viticultural possibilities in the 1600s, successfully planting in the Hudson River region. An innovative and forward-thinking farmer, Andrew Jackson Caywood became an expert on grape growing and cross breeding varieties, drawing attention and granting legitimacy to the strength of the agricultural region. In 1957, the Millers purchased Caywood's land and continued to nurture the thriving hybrids. Holding the first farm license in the United States, the Millers knew that something was special about this property; the appeal of the land was as strong as its history.

Top Left: Winemaker Kristop Brown brings years of experience to the Benmarl production.

Middle Left: Nicholas and Victor Spaccarelli Jr., with their dog Zeland, live and work on the vineyard.

Bottom Left: A close look at the Benmarl angel shows just how much Old World charm lives in the winery.

Facing Page: The tasting room and gift shop let everyone leave with a tasteful souvenir.

With Gaelic heritage, the Millers named the winery Benmarl, meaning slate hill in old Scottish tongue. It seemed perfect for the rich, southeastern slopes of the vineyards. Wine lovers and historians now flock to the winery to see the sights and taste the flavor of the land, particularly baco noir, made by the premier grape of the same name. Baco Noir won the Cornell Cup for Best Wine in the Hudson River Region, in addition to a number of other awards over the last half century. Traminette, made from hearty, cold-resistant grapes, is a favorite among visitors, as well as riesling, merlot, syrah and frontenac. Aged in oak, or stainless steel for fruit-forward whites, the wines are all artisan-made under the watchful eye of winemaker Kristop Brown and assistant winemaker and general manager Matthew Spaccarelli. More like a family than a staff, the team also includes 30-year veteran Linda Zambito as assistant to the general manager, jack-of-all-tradesman Ted Baker and educational coordinator Wendy Crispell.

Benmarl is a gem in New York's wine country, bringing together all the romance associated with Old World vineyards. The microclimate, slope, 400-foot elevation, and proximity to the river attribute to the minimal use of pesticides and sustainable growing practices while producing quality wines. Visitors get a peek at the local fauna when visiting, an exciting element of the growing habitat. Hummingbirds, butterflies and

Top Left: Quite a few of the wines have won the Cornell Cup and other awards—an impressive group of vintages.

Middle Left: The Spaccarelli family includes Stephen, Victor, Sarah and Matthew.

Bottom Left: The tasting bar offers a living portrait of the Hudson Valley and Berkshires.

Facing Page: Containing bottles from every vintage to date, the wine library shows off years of hard work.

migratory fowl make regular appearances. The original owner of the winery married an architect; and she later designed the building that fits perfectly into the Hudson River landscape, attracting local birds and wildlife. Burgundian in inspiration, the winery shows off antique baskets, cellar candles and old-fashioned glasses with the original logo. No detail of Benmarl's history is forgotten. Combine that nostalgia with nature, visitor events and unforgettable wine, and it becomes clear why Benmarl has been such a success for so many years.

BENMARL
WINERY
BACO NOIR

2007 | Hudson River Region

WINE & FARE

Baco Noir
Pairs perfectly with roast duck or roast pork, served alongside a savory peppercorn sauce.

Traminette
Suggested for pairing with vindaloo, Thai foods and wasabi-based dishes.

Slate Hill White
Pair with a variety of dishes. Try it with New York goat cheeses, grilled shrimp and lighter fare.

Tastings
Open to the public daily, year-round

Brotherhood, America's Oldest Winery

Washingtonville

As the nation's oldest operating winery with the largest underground, French oak cellars, Brotherhood Winery has bragging rights that most American businesses would kill for. And yet one visit to the Washingtonville location reveals the winery's humble demeanor and warm history, without a trace of ego.

Brotherhood's beginnings come from Jean Jaques, a French Huguenot who started in the boot making trade while living in Europe. Once arriving in America, Jean began planting vines in 1810. As a respected elder of the Presbyterian Church, Jean thought winemaking would be the perfect skill to offer his parishioners. More than four decades later, Jean's three sons—John Jr., Oren and Charles—received the operation in their father's will and dubbed the church Jaques Brothers' Winery. The youngest of the boys, Charles, placed the establishment in the hands of James and Edward Emerson upon his death. Bringing the region refreshing new flavors, James and Edward hailed from Armenia. The proprietors added two important elements that have been defining factors in the winery's character: the name Brotherhood and the extensive underground cellars. Many buildings from this period remain on the property today.

Top Left: Captured in 1891, a photograph reveals Brotherhood's main offices on the corner of Spring and Washington Street in New York, New York.
Photograph courtesy of Brotherhood Archives

Middle Left: Brotherhood executive offices also sat in New York that same year.
Photograph courtesy of Brotherhood Archives

Bottom Left: Washingtonville housed the champagne finishing area at the turn of the century, the same town where Brotherhood Winery remains today.
Photograph courtesy of Brotherhood Archives

Facing Page: The underground cellar, excavated by hand through the mid and late 1800s, shows the original cuvée casks, which are a part of Brotherhood's tour.
Photograph by Tomas Donoso

Louis Farrell and his son Louis Jr. took over the winery during the industry's toughest blow. Through the years of Prohibition until after World War II, the Farrell family kept the operation afloat by producing sacramental wines for the Catholic Church—a duty that allowed the title as oldest operating winery to survive. Louis Farrell began the idea of offering tours to visitors, opening up the world of winemaking to interested folks. His Columbia education and marketing career with Macy's gave him the perfect tools to spread his plans, revolutionizing the way the American public thinks of wineries. He let people feel like they were a part of something and showed off wine's appeal. And the 1960s' society could not get enough. Louis would send out invitations to parties, letting guests leave with cases of wine to spread notions of winery fun.

Top Right: Rip Van Winkle Vineyard in Hudson takes its name from a familiar character in American folklore.

Bottom Right: From left, the board of directors appear outside the of the winery: Juan Pablo Castro, Luis Chadwick, Cesar Baeza, Pablo Castro, Hernan Donoso and Francisco Chadwick.

Facing Page Top: The cask room and champagne vault hold the Grand Monarque Champagne in tirage.
Photograph by Yasuo Ota

Facing Page Bottom Left: The entrance to Grand Monarque Hall allures visitors with certain charm.

Facing Page Bottom Right: Grand Monarque Hall and Brotherhood courtyard are best enjoyed on a sunny day.
Photograph by Yasuo Ota

Since 2005, Cesar Baeza, with successful agri-businessmen Pablo Castro and Luis Chadwick, from his native country Chile, have owned Brotherhood. Cesar began with the company in the early 1970s and returned to run the show in 1987. The interim offered him opportunities worldwide with PepsiCo, Inc., where he worked for the wine and spirits division in charge of research and development. These acquired skills would become handy once returning to Brotherhood—the winery was ready to move from spiced wine and sweet blends to high-end, premium wines. And Cesar made this happen. Single handedly transforming aged barrels of chardonnay into a sought-after blend of 25 percent four-year-old chardonnay with 75 percent younger cabernet, he grabbed the wine world's attention with his Mariage, the "marriage" of two most noble grapes. Mariage became a collector's wine with his limited edition silver-etched bottles. Sparkling wine, pinot noir, merlot, cabernet sauvignon, chardonnay and riesling have also made a splash with connoisseurs and enthusiasts.

Top Left: The coat of arms for the Llado family—the surname of Mrs. Farrell's father—guards the gated iron vault containing some of the oldest vintages in Brotherhood's collection.
Photograph by Tomas Donoso

Middle Left: A crusher, which was used by the Jaques Brothers Winery, is on display in the museum section of the cellars.
Photograph by Tomas Donoso

Bottom Left: Brotherhood's gated cellar holds the winery's oldest vintages.
Photograph by Yasuo Ota

Facing Page: Current vintages age in French and American oak barrels.

The nostalgia of Brotherhood's past is very much alive at the winery. Flemish architecture, stone buildings and stepped roofs harken to the days of its inception. Antique lights from Grand Central Station, standing chimneys and exposed brick take visitors back to the simpler times of the 19th century, wine in hand. Brotherhood, under its new progressive international ownership, is undergoing a renaissance of sorts with major renovations aimed at restoring the grandeur of the only winery in the United States designated as a historical landmark.

Brotherhood
EST. 1839 ™
AMERICA'S OLDEST WINERY

Pinot Noir

New York Premium Selection

European emigre, Jean Jaques, produced Brotherhood's first commercial vintage in 1839, and the winery has been in continuous operation since that time.

WINE & FARE

Blanc de Blancs Champagne

All celebrations are enhanced by sparkling wine, but Brotherhood Blanc de Blancs is also a perfect aperitif, and pairs very well with raw bar items, light appetizers and brunch.

Riesling

Perfect as an aperitif or with salads, and an excellent accompaniment to any spicy dish, especially Asian foods— also superb with sushi and sashimi.

Pinot Noir

Brotherhood's Pinot Noir complements everything from salmon to chicken, veal to beef, and pairs perfectly with any dish that features mushrooms. Excellent with cheeses such as Brie, Jarlsberg and aged Cheddar.

Cabernet Sauvignon

Pairs with beef roasts, steaks, lamb chops, ragu sauces and other rich, hearty fare. Good aging potential.

Tastings

Open to the public daily, year-round

Millbrook Vineyards & Winery

Millbrook

Millbrook Vineyards & Winery encompasses the experiences of New York's Hudson River Valley; history, taste, agriculture and family meet here. If travelers had only one day to spend in the region, this would be the place to visit.

The winery's initial plantings began more than two decades ago, when John and Kathe Dyson took a chance on chardonnay, pinot noir, cabernet franc and tocai friulano. These four grape varieties have remained a stronghold for Millbrook, proving themselves as the company's mainstays year-in and year-out. No vinifera varietals have thrived in the Hudson River Valley environment quite like them. John and Kathe quickly saw their vineyards' potential and have shared their viticultural education with the world; the winery produces as many as 12,000 cases annually.

John and Kathe began with an old abandoned Millbrook dairy farm in 1981 and the region's wine industry has not been the same since. As the vinifera grapes flourished, the couple slowly began remodeling and converting the farm into top-notch vineyards, revealing the initial vintage in 1985. Since opening the region's first all-vinifera vineyard, and now the largest at 30 acres, the Dysons have remained perpetually involved in both the community and state and local public service. After serving as Agricultural Commissioner and Commissioner of Commerce for New York State where John started the "I Love NY" promotional campaign, John went on to serve as Deputy Mayor with Rudolph Giuliani where he oversaw the rejuvenation of New York City's economy. Actively engaged in local events, Kathe devotes her time to multiple charitable organizations and taking care of their grandchildren.

Top Left: White, red, rosé and dessert—Millbrook has wines for every course.

Bottom Left: Proprietor John S. Dyson stays perpetually involved with the community, through his personal and professional life, as well as through the winery.
Photograph by Harvey Klein

Facing Page: Seeing the vineyards at bud break is just as much of a reason to visit Millbrook as the wine itself.

Well drained soils, hillside trellising and close attention to viticultural detail makes winemaker and vineyard manager John Graziano's life most demanding. When cared for properly, the Hudson River microclimate is ideal for vinifera grapes. Westerly and southerly facing slopes keep the sun-exposed fruit available to the cool air, preventing an excess of moisture while developing distinctly Hudson Valley grape flavors. Cool, crisp and well balanced, Millbrook wines take on the taste of the geography. With impressive views of the Catskills—and a unique growing location, the Millbrook Winery site is second-to-none.

Local personality shines, evidenced by the array of events that bring the community together at Millbrook Winery—organized by vice president and general manager David Bova. From May to November, the second-floor tasting room, once a hay loft, in the Dutch-hipped barn converts to an art gallery, hosting Art in the Loft. The exhibit features works

of regional artists for both viewing and sale. Columbus Day weekend in October sees the annual harvest party, welcoming 350 people to feast beneath the autumn sky. New York City chefs arrive to prepare wine-friendly fare, taking advantage of the regional agriculture while spreading local tourism.

Above Left: Millbrook Winery tasting room is set in a warm loft with wood floors; plenty of sunlight keeps the room filled with good cheer.

Above Right: An art gallery gives guests more to think about than just the wine.

Facing Page: The winery's retail store and tasting room lets visitors buy a bottle of wine after sampling—the perfect gift for nearly any occasion.

A focus on quality wine and a dedicated promotion of the Hudson River Valley region has given Millbrook Winery its reputation, prompting *Hudson Valley Magazine* readers to vote it as the number one winery, 16 years running.

PROPRIETOR'S SPECIAL RESERVE
CABERNET FRANC
HUDSON RIVER REGION

WINE & FARE

Tocai Friulano
(100% tocai friulano)
This classic aperitif pairs well with Asian cuisine and seafood.

Chardonnay Proprietor's Special Reserve
(100% chardonnay)
Pair with roast chicken, shellfish or pasta with creamy sauces.

Pinot Noir Proprietor's Special Reserve
(100% pinot noir)
Pair with anything from roast chicken and grilled seafood to mild meat dishes—a great cross-over wine that can be served with a variety of foods.

Cabernet Franc Proprietor's Special Reserve
(85% cabernet franc, 15% merlot)
Spicy and robust, this wine is perfect with grilled or roasted meats such as filet mignon, venison and New York Strip steak.

Tastings
Open to the public daily, year-round

Stoutridge Vineyard

Marlboro

As proud stewards of the land in the Hudson Valley, Stephen Osborn and Kimberly Wagner opened Stoutridge Vineyard to share their enthusiasm with the public. Under a conscious effort to preserve and promote regional viticulture, the winery operates with a slow wine approach, refraining from mechanical processing and letting the grapes speak for themselves.

Stoutridge Vineyard promotes the region through agritourism and farm-centric wines. Opening in 2001, the winery has emphasized nature's bounty through minimal intervention. Three vineyards make up the Stoutridge property, focusing on German whites and Northern Italian reds. Varieties include riesling, pinot noir, teroldego, refosco, muscat, pinot blanc and sangiovese.

Stoutridge is run and built with respect to its surroundings, keeping the environment and sustainability in mind while holding quality as the top priority. Taking its cue from German vintners, the winery itself was built into a hillside on the site of a pre-Prohibition-era winery. The architecture capitalizes on geothermal energy and takes advantage of its east-facing orientation. Gravity techniques replace energy-eating pumping mechanisms to minimize disturbance and maintain flavor. In the winter months, radiant heating produced from energy reclaimed from the distillation process warms public spaces. For filtering sweet wines and distillates, Stephen and Kimberly have chosen an eco-friendly filtration process. Instead of using the more common methods of diatomaceous earth or paper filtering, which produces industrial waste, they have opted to use a cross-flow filter,

Top Left: Stephen Osborn takes breaks from long vineyard hours atop a traditional 750-gallon aging cask.

Bottom Left: The award-winning, colorful labels are as distinctive as the flavor of Stoutridge wines.

Facing Page: The design of the winery blends perfectly with its natural environment.

Top: The expansive tasting room comfortably accommodates both large and small groups.

Bottom: A state-of-the-art lab is used to monitor wine and distillate production from beginning to end.

Top: Always efficient, Stoutridge's underground barrel room maintains ideal aging conditions with no energy input.

Bottom: To capture the local flavor, the distillery incorporates three German artisan pot stills for maximum flexibility.

which produces biodegradable waste. Having the largest photovoltaic solar energy system in the county—33 kilowatts—and an involvement with a sustainability study at Cornell University, Stoutridge is doing its fair share of conservation.

With so many small wine-grape farms in the Hudson Valley, Stephen and Kimberly felt they had an opportunity to capture their local flavor; 90 percent of the wines result from local grapes. Each season, Stephen chooses a few farms and uses their grapes—the bottles contain 100 percent of the farm's produce. Richard Fino's farm in nearby Milton has supplied the fruit to create Vino Fino, a rich dark wine. The Fino farm has taken to planting more contemporary varietals, bringing forth an unfiltered, forward-looking wine with a sweet—not heavy—old-fashion flavor. Exhibiting a cross-section of each farms' varietals, the featured wines have as much personality as the farmers they come from.

Stephen was involved with lobbying at the state level to help pass the 2007 Farm Distillery Act. Since Stoutridge has an on-site distillery, Stephen and Kimberly wanted to sell the product directly to visitors. Now—just like a New York State farm winery—the distillery offers tastings, tours and purchasing opportunities. Benefiting all parties involved, the new law has been successful in bringing out the flavors of Upstate New York.

Above: The foundation wall from the original 1902 winery has been incorporated into the tasting room patio.
Photograph by Stephen Osborn

Facing Page: A young vineyard takes advantage of the frost protection given by a farm pond.

The history of the Stoutridge property is as rich as the philosophy it holds. Since its purchase, the property has flourished under Stephen and Kimberly's care. The team has an all-encompassing, hands-on approach that keeps them connected to the history, the land and most importantly, the wine.

WINE & FARE

Hudson Heritage
(75% sevyal blanc)

Pair with shellfish and simply prepared fish.

Quimby's Rose
(old-fashion farm blend)

Pair with classic German foods, mustard and sausage.

Vino Fino
(modern rural farm blend with frontenac and dechaunac)

Pair with an array of lamb dishes and stews.

Vidal
(100% vidal)

Pair with seafood in rich cream sauces; casseroles; chicken with complex preparations.

Tastings
Open to the public Friday through Sunday, year-round

Warwick Valley Winery & Distillery

Warwick

Blend the high quality standards of a European château, the freshness of a local farm and the casual and friendly atmosphere of a favorite pub. The result: Warwick Valley Winery & Distillery, started in 1994. The wines, ciders and fruit brandies make Warwick Valley Winery a unique gem in the picturesque Hudson Valley.

Warwick Valley Winery & Distillery offers much more than just wine. The winery's flagship product, Doc's Draft Hard Cider has received international recognition as a top-tier hard cider. Using only the finest apples, pears and raspberries, Warwick Valley Winery has created a premier hard cider from estate-grown and locally sourced fruit.

In 2001 the winery added a distillery to its list of endeavors and is now producing a line of fruit brandies and liqueurs. Whole-fruit fermentation followed by a slow distillation results in Warwick Valley Winery & Distillery's exceptional fruit brandies. The American Fruits line of distilled spirits capture the essence of the fruit and are reminiscent of the finest French and German fruit brandies.

Top Left: The winery road-front sign at the entrance welcomes guests.

Bottom Left: The view of the distillery doors, walking from the orchard toward the winery, shows off unmistakable charm.

Facing Page: One peek of the pond, pear orchard, stables and the back of the winery and distillery draws in traffic from the roadside; everyone wants to visit.

The winery also produces a variety of delicious wines. They range from the fun and fruit-forward Black Dirt Red, named after the area's rich and fertile soil, to the award-winning vinifera varietals including cabernet franc, riesling and chardonnay. With more than a dozen wines, Warwick Valley Winery & Distillery can please any palate.

If the wines, ciders and fruit brandies are not enough, the winery offers apple and pear picking in season. The orchards that surround the tasting room are filled with over 30 varieties. Pickers get the option of choosing heritage varieties like golden russet and new spectacular varieties like honeycrisp and fortune.

Top Left: A collection of Warwick Valley signature ciders, brandies and liqueurs give tasters a less-traditional sampling of what the winery has to offer.

Middle Left: The tasting bar prominently displays the winery's ciders.

Bottom Left: For the most tempting smells in the house, visitors should head toward the dining room and entrance to the bakery and café, Pané.

Facing Page: Looking out from the top of the orchard, eyes gaze at Mount Adam and Eve—appropriately named.

The final piece to an exceptional experience is Pané, the winery's bakery and café. Pizza, salads and great gourmet sandwiches are available Fridays, Saturdays and Sundays from 12 to five in the evening. Eat, drink and be merry—Warwick Valley Winery & Distillery has got simplicity down to an art.

WARWICK VALLEY

WINERY & DISTILLERY

WINE & FARE

Riesling
Pair this with a favorite spicy Asian cuisine or the winery's salmon and Brie pizza.

Doc's Draft Hard Apple Cider
Pair with any pub fare or grilled pork chops.

Cabernet Franc
Pair with goat cheese, lamb or venison.

Black Currant Cordial
Mix with Doc's Hard Cider, Prosecco or vodka.

Tastings
Open to the public daily, year-round

Atwater Estate Vineyards, *page 136*
Photograph by Katie Marks

Hermann J. Wiemer Vineyard, *page 190*

Finger Lakes

Americana Vineyards & Winery

Interlaken

A sense of family pervades Americana Vineyards & Winery as soon as visitors walk through the door. It is a place for friendship. "That's what we're all about," says president and owner Joe Gober. "We're special because our focus is on quality, service and community." Regulars come back year after year from all over the country because they know they will get great wine, great service and great food. What more could they want?

Housed in an 1820s' swing barn, Americana is the epitome of comfort and home. The building was saved from demolition in 1999 with a little help from the New York State Historical Society. "It was too beautiful and too important to let it go," says vice president and co-owner Nancy Wright. The barn was carefully dismantled piece by piece and rebuilt at its current location in Interlaken. Nearly two centuries later, the building houses Americana's tasting room and gift shop.

Customer service is another obvious point of pride for Americana. Tasting room manager Leslie Lankford is passionate about training her staff—customers are assured the very best information. Everyone is greeted with a friendly hello and encouraged to step right up to the tasting bar for a sampling of up to 16 wines. The traditional semidry riesling is a must; it finishes with hints of honey and apricot and touts the New York State Fair's double gold and New York Wine & Food Classic gold seals of excellence. Reintroducing people to Finger Lakes wine, Americana is excited about the incredible time for the region. Joe knows that "everything is getting better, and we're at the forefront."

Top Left: Max and Rubie—the chocolate Labradors—greet visitors at the tasting room entrance.

Bottom Left: Complete your taste of the Americana experience with fresh, comfortable fare in The Crystal Lake Café.

Facing Page: Warm hospitality abounds in the splendor of the circa-1820s restored barn, housing the tasting room and gift shop.

Forefront indeed. This multiple-award-winning winery offers something for every palate. Just as the seasons of the Finger Lakes have their own special characteristics, so do the wines of Americana. The dog days of summer beg for the crisp Cayuga White; lakeside sunsets in autumn are savored with fruity November Harvest; winter evenings warmed with peppery Cabernet Franc; spring time blooms with Barn Raising Red.

The Crystal Lake Café, led by executive chef Lindsay Freeman, is Americana's newest addition. The restaurant's mission is to create comfortable dishes from fresh, seasonal ingredients—it's an honest reflection of the Finger Lakes region, featuring local cheese and produce. Chef Stan Walton and artisan baker Jen Ungberg round out a professional kitchen staff that is committed to creating a menu from whole ingredients. Stan and Jen stand by the notion that if it can be made in-house, it should be. Fresh baked breads, cured and smoked meats, desserts, chutneys, relishes—even ketchup—nothing is out of reach.

For those with a sweet tooth, homemade chocolate fudge will top the list; Americana boasts more than 30 delicious varieties. Although Julie Blodgett—who makes fudge weekly with Nancy and Diana Poyer— loves the pumpkin pie flavor, the chocolate peanut butter and wine berry made with baco noir are universal favorites.

Top Left: Wine for every palate and season awaits visitors.

Middle Left: Welcome to Americana Vineyards & Winery.

Bottom Left: Springtime reveals some of the vineyards' most beautiful—and flavorful—offerings.

Facing Page: Relax the day away overlooking the pond and vineyards.

Things are growing outside the winery as well, with presence in more than 100 retail stores and restaurants in New York state, thanks largely to the efforts of wholesale manager Billy Oeschlin. And calls come in daily. They ship "anywhere the law allows," Joe adds with a smile.

Whatever the season, if you're looking for a friendly destination, a great glass of wine and a comfortable meal, this is the place for a true taste of Americana. Max and Rubie—the chocolate labs that are the true owners—are ready to greet.

WINE & FARE

Americana White
(Catawba)

Pair this gold-winning white with a Cajun burger or Asian foods.

Baco Noir

Serve with grilled veggies and red or white meats —a full-bodied, deep red Burgundy.

Cayuga White

Pair with sharp cheese. Perfect for a picnic, this is a semi-dry, all-purpose selection.

Sweet Rosie

Serve with chocolate-covered strawberries, cheesecake or homemade fudge.

Tastings
Open to the public daily, year-round

Atwater Estate Vineyards

Hector

W ith enough personality to entertain all of New York, the Marks family owns and operates Atwater Estate Vineyards, bringing all of their appeal to the winery. So grab a glass of wine and have a seat—everyone is family.

Responding to the 1976 Winery Act, Atwater began as Rolling Vineyards, situated on the southeastern edge of Seneca Lake. Ted Marks bought the property and opened it to the public in 2000, spreading the vineyards and adding a functional winery with a new name. Previously, cattle and fruit orchards ruled the land, growing some of the country's sweetest peaches and cherries as late as 1930. Catawba, Niagara and Concord grapes are indigenous to the region, present since the Iroquois tended the land hundreds of years ago. Atwater now concentrates on vinifera grapes and French-American hybrids, producing signature blends, dessert, white and red wines. Most notably, Atwater's wines have been honored with the Best North American Riesling award in an Australian competition, gaining fans around the world.

Top Left: Guests are welcomed to the tasting room by a grand copper door handle crafted by local blacksmith Durand Van Doren.
Photograph by Sheryl Sinkow

Bottom Left: Fresh-cut flowers from the cutting garden grace the wooden wine racks inside the quaint tasting room.

Facing Page: Warm and inviting, the tasting room is a converted early 20th-century cattle barn, surrounded by mature gardens and incredible views of the lake.
Photograph by Katie Marks

Over the years, the Marks family has watched the Finger Lakes region boom—a 4,000-square-mile space with 11 ice age-carved lakes. As Katie Marks leads public relations, the family strongly promotes the area and its infinite virtues. Atwater sits on the Seneca Lake Wine Trail: a collection of the region's strongest wineries, ranging from boutique to high-volume. The trail creates camaraderie amongst the lakeshore neighbors and gives tourists the opportunity to see what the area really has to offer. A 10-mile stretch of New York wine country—endearingly termed the Banana Belt—has produced more Governors' Cup Awards than anywhere else in the state. Earning itself a series line in the Atwater family, the Banana Belt has been coined because of its relatively warmer weather in comparison to the surrounding region. Deceptively free of banana cultivation, the land boasts perfect growing conditions for some of the state's highest quality vines, incubating the grapes during harsh Northeastern winters.

Top Left: Looking south towards Watkins Glen, the deck offers a magnificent place to enjoy sipping wine while overlooking the vineyards and Seneca Lake.
Photograph by Katie Marks

Middle Left: Atwater's lineup includes a dry sparkling wine and dessert ice wine, beautifully packaged in its signature silk screened labels.

Bottom Left: Planted with 15 varieties of grapes on over 50 acres, the vineyards are spectacular throughout every season.
Photograph by Katie Marks

Facing Page: While nestled deep in the vineyards, guests enjoy an evening of fine wine and local food served during the summer's Vine Dining series.
Photograph by Dylan Buyskes

What is the best way to experience the region? Vineyard-set dinner parties on warm summer evenings would be a good place to start. Every year, Atwater sets the table for 24, inviting guests to eat locally sourced cuisine prepared tableside by regional chefs. During the intimate and informative event, guests listen to vintners' commentary from winemaker Vincent Aliperti while sampling five memorable courses and chatting with connoisseurs, tourists, gourmets and locals. Year-round, the winery has events and functions to entertain wine and food lovers. Relaxed, warm and perpetually inviting, Atwater is the perfect way to experience the Finger Lakes.

WINE & FARE

Cabernet Franc

*Savor this fruit-forward red with roast chicken, braised meats
wand soft, aromatic cheeses.*

Dry Riesling

*Crisp and fresh, this wine pairs well with grilled shrimp,
scallops and semi-soft cheese.*

Late Harvest Vignoles

*Enjoy this luscious dessert wine as an aperitif with blue
cheese and figs, or sip after a meal alongside fresh peaches.*

Tastings

Open to the public daily, year-round

Belhurst Winery

Geneva

Romance, legends and luxury—Belhurst Winery offers all that a true castle should, plus more. Fulfilling the expectations that the word castle evokes, Belhurst Winery delivers a double dose of old-world splendor with an award-winning winery accompanying the grand quarters, all on the shores of Seneca Lake in Geneva, New York.

Because of its history, the winery's folkloric charm and mystery has stayed with the home, giving guests a memorable tale to recount. Before European contact, the land was inhabited by the Council of the Six Nations of Iroquois. This began the long tale of the Belhurst property, changing hands from one colorful character to the next through the years, eventually landing safely in the lap of Duane Reeder in 1992. The 19th century saw the private residence inhabited by a reclusive embezzler from Britain's Covent Garden Theater, then by Carrie M. Young Herron in 1885. Carrie was a young New York City woman who left her husband to marry her manager, Captain Louis Dell Collins. Made almost entirely of European imports, the new four-story manor was erected by Mrs. Collins. The home took four years to build with the dedication of 50 men. So laborious was the process, two construction workers gave the ultimate sacrifice—one man fell from the tower and another lost his mind while installing the roof.

In addition to a namesake blush wine, Carrie's contribution to Belhurst has been immortalized through the love of her two most prized possessions during her years at Belhurst: a pair of golden pheasants. Golden Pheasant has become a highly acclaimed wine, a luscious semi-sweet blend of sevyal and chardonnay with a nose of ripe, sweet apple blossoms.

Top Left: The Neptune mosaic overlooks the fireplace in the great hall. Original jaunty statues sit on the hand-carved, wooden mantels that were built with Belhurst.

Bottom Left: Carrie Collins, the original builder of Belhurst, was a woman ahead of her time. She often threw elaborate parties and had golden pheasants strolling her lawns.

Facing Page: The front of the winery shows the hand-cut, red Medina stone that makes up the exterior of the castle. Many bedrooms offer lake views and balconies.
Photograph by John Francis McCarthy

Upon acquiring Belhurst in 1932, Cornelius J. Dwyer, or Red, operated the home as a speakeasy, casino and bar. His wild and wooly ways attracted friends from across the country, funneling in liquor from Canada. With the dull days of Prohibition upon the country, word of Belhurst spread under the ownership of Red—making its name synonymous with luxury and merriment. The gambling and booze later subsided, leaving behind unbridled potential for the home's future. The bootlegger's legend is found on the Belhurst label for its vintage Red, a casual, velvety wine.

Belhurst's reputation has added elegant romance to its character over the years, transforming into a wine-lovers getaway. Surrounded by vineyards, the Reeders have expanded Belhurst under Duane's care with his son Kevin as general manager and president. The family augmented the lodgings, adding the modern Vinifera Inn onto the original 14-roomed Chambers in Belhurst Castle. White Springs Manor, a Georgian revival farm mansion, sits amidst vineyards just two miles east. A wine tasting room and retail shop let connoisseurs peruse selections while ample ballroom space offers a venue for galas, weddings and events. Duane saw a market for his winery-hotel hybrid when wineries began to far outnumber lodgings and restaurants in the Finger Lakes region. Travelers need a place to stay and good wine needs great food. So, he traded in grape growing for his wine steering committee—a group of experts who seek out growers and guide the product line at Belhurst.

Top Left: Vinifera Inn's rooms face Seneca Lake and offer fireplaces and Jacuzzis.

Middle Left: Edgar's bar reveals all hand-carved woodwork, marble and a mirror-adorned working fireplace.

Bottom Left: Belhurst wines can be purchased from the wine and gift shop.

Facing Page: The outdoor fire pit attracts guests, gathering to chat with good wine in hand.

Stonecutters is one of two dining options at Belhurst, serving casual, eclectic tavern fare. Besides the unbeatable views of the lake, a massive stone fireplace, sunken bar and outdoor fire pit attract guests. For upscale cuisine in a decadent setting, Edgar's reigns supreme—beamed cathedral ceilings and aged chestnut adorn the interior. Mosaic-tiled fireplaces appear throughout, most notably in the great hall where the embellishment has garnered a white wine named in its honor, Neptune. *Wine Spectator* recognizes Edgar's wine list, giving the restaurant its Award of Excellence 13 times and adding accolades to their 40-plus awards. A gem in the Finger Lakes, the winery is full of personality, life and romance, aptly voted one of the most romantic places in New York State.

WINE & FARE

Belhurst Cayuga

Serve as a wonderful accompaniment with light cream-based herb sauces, quiche and mild appetizers.

Belhurst Merlot

Pair with filet mignon, venison, grilled or roasted beef and other spicy dishes.

Neptune

Pair this fruit-forward white blend with seafood Newburg, Asian dishes, grilled chicken kebabs, fruit salad and broiled cod fish.

Tastings
Open to the public daily, year-round

Bully Hill was founded in 1970 by fourth-generation vintner Walter S. Taylor. Walter's family established the Taylor Wine Company in 1883 and maintained it successfully through Prohibition by labeling the grape juice with strict instructions of how not to make wine; generations later the thriving enterprise was acquired by The Coca-Cola Company. Walter became a vintner through family roots—but he was also an artist, an outspoken man with a distinct sense of humor, often known to voice his opinion, which was how Bully Hill got started.

Walter felt that New York State had the capacity to produce 100-percent, locally derived wine without additives, despite the fact that only 53 percent of regional grapes were required to become genuine New York wine. During this time, many area wines were irreverently called tank car wine. When juice was ordered from other major wine producing regions like California, a means of transportation had to be devised. Grapes were de-stemmed and crushed prior to being shipped, which negatively altered the taste. The affected juice was pumped into rail cars and shipped from the West Coast for a 3,000-mile journey, resulting in the infamous "tank car wine." This is the practice that Walter spoke unreservedly against—in fact, he was so opposed to the transport practice that he purchased a 40-ton tank car and planted it right in the middle of his own vineyards.

Walter and his father Greyton planted French-American hybrid grapes including baco noir and marechal foch, which are best-suited to western New York's terroir than most types of viniferous grapes. He took his idea to the next level and produced a red wine made from

Top Left: Colobel is one of the many grape varieties found on the Bully Hill Estate.
Photograph by Sean King

Bottom Left: Bully Hill Pinot Grigio ranks as a top favorite among visitors.
Photograph by Sean King

Facing Page: Chancellor and noir are some of the oldest vines on the estate—easily seen from the wine tasting room.
Photograph by Sean King

Above: Served more than any other, Love My Goat is best paired with fresh-ingredient fare. The flavor falls between dry and sweet—perfect with the Maryland crab cakes and seared scallops over a tender portobello mushroom.
Photographs by Sean King

Left: Bully Hill Restaurant features innovative cuisine while overlooking the beautiful Keuka Lake.
Photograph by Sean King

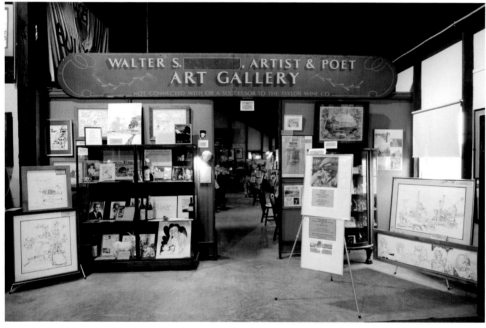

his hybrid grapes grown alongside Keuka Lake. After conducting a tasting of this new production compared to earlier Taylor wines in 1967, it faired as a superior vintage, much to the dismay of the Taylors' board of trustees. Although Walter was subsequently let go, this maverick entrepreneur was hugely inspired to expand upon his 100-percent New York State grapes concept and in 1970 Bully Hill opened its doors. The red wine Walter produced created excitement and Walter's Estate Red was born; it remains one of Bully Hill Vineyards' most appreciated, complex and heavy-bodied red wines.

Today, Bully Hill vintners produce more than 250,000 cases of wine annually. In addition to producing its own estate-grown grapes, the winery is the largest purchaser of grapes from the Finger Lakes region. All vintages are made exclusively from New York State grapes without the complication of water or other additives. The winery is privately owned and operated by Walter's wife Lillian Taylor, who spends much of her time overseeing Bully Hill's seasonal restaurant. The estate vineyard restaurant features a wide variety of innovative cuisine from its signature Maryland crab cakes to more traditional barbecue dishes. Visitors can dine on the deck to enjoy the vineyard view or savor the menu in a relaxed atmosphere indoors.

Top Left: Winemaker and vice president Gregg Learned has been the winemaker since 1981.

Middle Left: The Walter S. Taylor Art Gallery features over 200 original pieces of work by the namesake artist, founder of Bully Hill Vineyards in 1970.

Bottom Left: Walter enjoyed the winery land with his beloved goat, Guilt Free.
Photograph courtesy of Bully Hill Vineyards, Inc.

Facing Page: A view of Keuka Lake from Bully Hill leaves a lasting impression.
Photograph by Sean King

A day trip to Bully Hill would not be complete without a stop at the tasting room where an unfiltered sense of humor is welcome and encouraged. Surrounded by its spirited atmosphere, one is apt to experience song, dance, laughter or a heavy one-ounce pour—or any combination thereof. As Walter once said, "At Bully Hill we always remember to laugh at ourselves, at adversity, at life…and never forget the importance of sometimes pressing grapes with our bare feet." Kristin Demaree, the tasting room host, has one hearty disclaimer: "We may be rowdy, we might be raucous, but there will be, without a doubt, cowboy hats involved!"

WINE & FARE

Estate Red
(baco noir, chancellor noir and chelois)

Pair with smoked beef brisket and spicy barbecue sauce on grilled ciabatta bread.

Love My Goat Red
(baco noir, marechal foch and aurore)

Pair with a grilled, black angus burger topped with bacon and swiss cheese.

Fish Market White
(seyval and vidal)

Pair with Maryland crab cake on a roasted portobello mushroom, smothered with pan-seared scallops.

Sweet Walter Rosé
(catawba and castel)

Pair with sliced oven-roasted turkey, lettuce, red onion, and cranberry mayo on ciabatta bread.

Tastings
Open to the public daily, year-round

Casa Larga Vineyards

Fairport

Walk into any home in Gaeta—a coastal Italian town in central Italy—and it becomes obvious why the culture is so closely linked with hospitality. "*Benvenuto! Beviamo!*" the host orders, lifting his glass to welcome newly arrived guests. Everyone is family.

This same attitude beams from Casa Larga Vineyards in Fairport, New York. And how could it not? Besides the fact that its welcoming name means "large house" in Italian, the winery's history begins in Gaeta with the Colaruotolo family. Andrew, the third son of four children, farmed the fields alongside his grandparents and tended to the family-run grocer's shop whenever he could. Not knowing it at the time, he would one day take his understanding of the land and virtues of the Italian food culture to America.

Traditionally, Italian farms are large plots of land divided into small parcels owned by a number of families. One family can easily own parcels in several regions, giving them an array of climates, topographies and food sources. The Colaruotolos had farms specializing in olives, cheese and lemons. Casa Larga, the farm where his grandmother hand-harvested grapes and made wine, was the most memorable for Andrew. Its distinguished reputation for high-grade grapes and superior wine made the farm an ideal inspiration for a namesake winery.

Andrew—or Mr. C as he was affectionately known—worked in architecture when he first came to the United States and kept up with grape growing on the side. Together with the encouragement of his wife Ann—Mrs. C—he planted the first vines for what would become Casa Larga Vineyards in 1974, with the first harvest following just four

Top Left: The founding family, from left: John Colaruotolo, Mary Jo Telesca, Ann Colaruotolo and Andrea Colaruotolo-O'Neill. They each help guide the winery according to family values and traditions.

Bottom Left: Andrew Colaruotolo and his wife Ann, or Mr. and Mrs. C, founded Casa Larga to produce wines reminiscent of those from his family's vineyard in Gaeta, Italy.
Photograph courtesy of Casa Larga Vineyards

Facing Page: The Italian-style winery and tasting room at Casa Larga sits atop Turk Hill, providing a breathtaking view of vineyards and rolling hills leading to Lake Ontario.

years later. As his dreams grew so did the vines. The establishment received its official license as the 21st winery in New York State, laying the groundwork for the industry's future.

The family opened their doors early on, inviting guests to taste their wines and experience a piece of the Mediterranean lifestyle. Casa Larga led the idea of establishing a stylish tasting room for guests to relax and enjoy wine and an Italian experience, as opposed to the cold production-facility settings of the early 1980s. This notion allowed all guests to feel as though they had been transported into a Mediterranean home, with keystone elliptical windows, pale stone exterior and the all-around appeal of an Italian villa. Although the swept-away surroundings added ambience, the wine spoke for itself—people loved it. The winery received a benchmark gold medal in 1980 for Riesling, reassuring the family that they were heading in the right direction.

Right: Fiori Vidal Ice Wine, produced using traditional German eiswein techniques, has been recognized as one of the highest rated ice wines in the United States.
Photograph courtesy of Casa Larga Vineyards

Facing Page Top: Bella Vista, the special events facility at the vineyard, is Upstate New York's premier venue for dream wine-country weddings.
Photograph courtesy of Casa Larga Vineyards

Facing Page Bottom Left: Italian heritage runs through every aspect of Casa Larga, where guests are welcomed as family and are encouraged to experience an Italian way of life.
Photograph courtesy of Casa Larga Vineyards

Facing Page Bottom Right: Casa Larga's CLV Chardonnay is grown and bottled in New York.
Photograph courtesy of Casa Larga Vineyards

More than 400 awards and eight grandchildren later, Mrs. C continues to guide the vision she and her husband shared. Her children are nearby; John is head winemaker and assists with all business matters, while Mary Jo serves as the head of finance and Andrea assists in developing the company's vision through marketing and day-to-day operations. Having the family in close proximity carries on Italian traditions and offers visitors exactly what they would expect from an Italian vineyard—warmth and generosity.

Serving 23 types of wine, Casa Larga grows two varietal classes: European vinifera and French-American hybrids. Within those two classes are five wine series: Fiori, Estate, Premium, Varietal and Artistic. From the usual suspects—merlot, cabernet franc, gewürztraminer, chardonnay—to the increasingly popular blends and ice wines, the series has a wide spectrum of flavors to bring to the table. A growing

favorite around the world, rich, nectar-like dessert wines of Casa Larga are beginning to win over American wine drinkers. The Fiori Vidal Ice Wine won the 2005 Governor's Cup for Best Wine in New York State from the New York Wine and Food Classic and the 2005 Fiori Cabernet Franc Ice Wine brought home double gold in the Taster's Guild International, attesting to its growing recognition as a world-class dessert wine.

Above Left: A sweeping view of the hilltop vineyards creates the perfect atmosphere for an outdoor wine tasting or special event.
Photograph courtesy of Casa Larga Vineyards

Above Right: Casa Larga's Pinor Noir is grown and bottled in New York. The terroir of the Finger Lakes wine region creates excellent conditions for high-quality pinot noir wines.
Photograph courtesy of Casa Larga Vineyards

Facing Page: Lush vines frame the image of Casa Larga's recognizable bell tower, a symbol of the winery's Italian heritage.
Photograph courtesy of Casa Larga Vineyards

Just as generations before them, this Colaruotolo generation believes in staying connected to the community. In addition to its popular annual events such as the Fire & Ice Festival and Purple Foot Grape Stomping Festival, Casa Larga is dedicated to contributing to local organizations with a focus on community and children, including organizations such as CURE Childhood Cancer Association and the National Center for Missing and Exploited Children.

With big hearts, open homes and fantastic wines, the Colaruotolo family welcomes visitors from around the world to join them at Casa Larga Vineyards and "experience an Italian way of life."

WINE & FARE

Casa Larga Fiori Vidal Ice Wine
(100% vidal)

Pair with decadent desserts such as cheesecake and crème brulée, or enjoy a glass on its own as an after-dinner drink.

Casa Larga Fiori Cabernet Franc Ice Wine
(100% cabernet franc)

Pair with luscious dark chocolate and dark desserts such as black forest cake. It is also fabulous on its own as a dessert.

Casa Larga Riesling
(100% riesling)

Pair with spicy Thai and Indian dishes.

Tastings
Open to the public daily, year-round

Constellation Brands

Victor

What if a corporation could maintain all the advantages of a big business and still possess the virtues of a small one? Constellation Brands has done just that. With the top spot as the world's largest wine company, this purveyor of quality alcohol beverages and sound business relationships stands strong.

Spanning the globe—North America, Europe, South Africa, Australia, New Zealand, Asia—Constellation Brands produces and/or markets beer, wine and spirits, with its home base in Upstate New York. Previously Canandaigua Wine Company, Constellation Wines U.S. now encompasses three wine businesses in the United States: Icon Estates, Centerra and VineOne. Organized to serve local markets, the company's decentralized management structure places discretion and authority with its regional management. Not only does this model bring quality wines to a range of geographies and consumer demographics, but it also provides advantages in every aspect throughout the Constellation organization. Constellation Wines North America CEO José Fernandez echoes the philosophy that his company practices, leaving decision making in the hands of those who know best—the longtime vintners and winemakers, as well as sales and marketing professions. Maintaining this entrepreneurial culture affords a rare benefit: big business has the global reach to spread local flavor.

Top Left: Glenn Curtis, Widmer's Wine Cellars general manager and winemaker, oversees the development and production of Widmer wines.

Bottom Left: Widmer's premium wines include Brickstone Cellars, 77 Days Riesling and Solaria Port. The winery produces more than 30 different types of wine.

Facing Page: The winery is located in Naples, New York, in the heart of the Finger Lakes region. Situated in a valley, the soil and cool climate make the area ideal for growing grapes.
Photograph by John Francis McCarthy

Top: John Jacob Widmer founded the winery out of his home in the late 1880s after coming to America in 1882 from Switzerland.

Bottom: Widmer's winery and Swiss Chalet tasting room attracts multitudes of visitors each year, especially during the fall foliage festivals in Upstate New York.

Top: The winery uses stainless steel lines to transfer wine to the bottling hall.

Bottom: Widmer operates five bottling lines. The wines are shipped throughout the Northeast and along the Atlantic Seaboard.

Personifying the American dream, Marvin Sands began his entrepreneurial endeavor just after naval service in World War II, 1945. With Russian immigrant grandparents, Marvin was one of the first males in his family born in the United States. Along with guiding principles from his mother and father, the spirit of the free market put the 21-year-old on the path to success. Buying a winery in New York's Finger Lakes region, Marvin, together with his eight-man crew sold bulk wine to bottlers. As the years passed, this small venture named Canandaigua Industries picked up steam—eventually reaching $5.2 billion in annual net sales with approximately 60 facilities around the world in fiscal 2007.

The corporation has achieved success by organic product growth and through acquiring its alcohol companies or brands and preserving their distinct personalities, including the high-profile purchases of BRL Hardy in 2003, Robert Mondavi in 2004, Vincor International in 2006 and Clos du Bois in 2007. Management allows wineries and distilleries to thrive by providing resources and financial support, much like Widmer's Wine Cellars on the south end of Canandaigua Lake at Naples, New York. The winery is now the state's oldest non-sacramental wine house with sales beginning in 1888. Constellation Brands produces 10 million cases per year in New York, making some of the region's most beloved wines: Arbor Mist, Manischewitz, Taylor New York and Richard's Wild Irish Rose.

Above Left: The entrance to the visitor's center at the Widmer winery is surrounded by the head of a 100-year-old oak cask.

Above Right: Widmer's Swiss Chalet tasting room was built from original field stone. Visitors to the winery can sample Niagara, chardonnay and riesling wines along with ports and sherries.

Facing Page: Part of the Canandaigua Wine Trail, Widmer's has events and activities for visitors throughout the year.

Whether situated in New Zealand, Canada or in New York, Constellation has dedicated itself to growing individual brands and improving the quality. Personality is key, whether for Inniskillin Icewine or SVEDKA Vodka. Each beverage has its own story and distinct potential; the skill comes in harvesting those qualities and delivering it to the public. Now focused on product premiumization, the company's heritage continues to chart the path of progress. Taking their mother Mickey's influence and following their father's open mind and business savvy, Richard and Rob now serve as chairman and chief executive officer, respectively. Upholding family ideals, the same values remain just as they did in 1945: entrepreneurial spirit, quality, integrity, customer focus and people.

Constellation

WINE & FARE

Widmer Lake Niagara Harvest Red

Lighter than most reds, this blend pairs well with an array of mild cheeses, baked olives, light Indian cuisine or spinach salads with fresh fruit.

Brickstone Cellars Chardonnay

Accompanies seared halibut prepared with leeks, haricot verts and a light lemon-garlic sauce. Also pairs well with braised, whole stuffed artichokes and straightforward pasta dishes.

Widmer Solaria Vintage Port

Pairs well with fresh Bartlett pear slices, Stilton cheese and toasted walnuts; duck breast with a cherry and port-wine reduction; or fresh strawberries with balsamic vinegar and cracked black pepper.

Tastings
Widmer's is open to the public daily, seasonally

Dr. Konstantin Frank's Vinifera Wine Cellars

Hammondsport

Konstantin Frank is a hero in the wine industry. His legacy remains the strongest in the Finger Lakes region and his story is best told by grandson Frederick, who now runs the family winery. The humble pride in Frederick's tone as he speaks of Konstantin reveals the character of the company.

Born in Ukraine, Konstantin came to America in 1951 with a strong education in viticulture. He possessed a PhD from the University of Odessa with thesis studies on the growth of Vitis vinifera in cold climates. Historically, this vine is found in southern Germany, France and Italy—all of which are warmer climates. While in New York, Dr. Frank accepted a position with the Geneva Experiment Station at Cornell University. Here, he advocated a progression toward the use of vinifera vines instead of the traditional native grapes used by the region's vineyards. The notion was met with doubt and cynicism from industry peers. Trusting his extensive knowledge of plant studies, Dr. Frank persisted in his belief of the superiority of vinifera fruit and opened Dr. Konstantin Frank's Vinifera Wine Cellars in 1962.

After continual obstacles from the root-eating insect phylloxera, Dr. Frank developed and revolutionized the growing of East Coast grapes through a grafting technique. He fused American rootstock with European scions, providing greater biocontrol of the plants. This allowed the crop to successfully grow in cold climates, yielding premium fruit to use for winemaking. Eager to share his understanding, Dr. Frank openly communicated his knowledge with regional winemakers, propagating the use of vinifera vines. Although it took some time, his methods finally caught on with local vintners, making Dr. Frank the driving force behind premium eastern American wines.

Top Left: Third-generation vintner Frederick Frank is grateful for the region's rich natural resources, allowing for world-class wines. Shale stone from the vineyard soil contributes to the wine's mineral terroir.

Middle Left: The entrance way into Dr. Frank's tasting room sees visitors from around the world—history buffs, wine enthusiasts and travelers, alike.

Bottom Left: Gewürztraminer grapes are ready for harvest in the fall, sweet and plump.

Facing Page: A favorite visitors' spot includes a view of the winery from the bluff.
Photograph by John Francis McCarthy

Top: No one would disagree—the view of the bluff on Keuka Lake is absolutely beautiful.

Bottom: With the changing of the leaves, fall is the best time to visit the vineyards.

Top: A revealing testament, Dr. Frank's tasting room is adorned with gold medal-winning wines.

Bottom: The grafted vines nursery overlooks Keuka Lake, a key component to creating the microclimate.

Years of winery work and attending the Cornell School of Agriculture prepared Frederick to take over as the third-generation president of the vineyard in 1993. With his cousin Eric Volz at his side as the vineyard manager, the two have kept up a strong family tradition of winemaking. They have assembled a trusted team to carry out production, hailing from around the globe. Antoine Boilley and Peter Weis—from French and German family wineries, respectively—bring in European expertise. Jonathon Luestner has also joined the team bringing Australian tradition. Mark Veraguth previously worked in Napa Valley with S. Anderson and studied at UC Davis, adding years of experience to the winemaking team. Eric Bauman oversees the production at Chateau Frank, a sister production facility built in 1860 that creates sparkling wine. These sparkling wines require at least seven years of aging prior to release, a longer fermentation time than most wines. Because of this, Eric takes advantage of the ideal cellars, set deep into the ground. The group also crafts wine for Salmon Run—a value line of wines at Dr. Frank's cellars.

New York soils have been highly conducive to growing the award-winning wines, including riesling, pinot gris, chardonnay, gewürztraminer, pinot noir and rkatsiteli. The cold climate has shifted from being viewed as a liability to an active asset, generating regional tasting notes. Although New York was selected as the location for Dr. Frank's vineyard because of its viticultural microclimate, it has also

Top Left: Dr. Frank's barrel cellar holds wines that have won both domestic and international awards.

Middle Left: Dr. Konstantin Frank arrived in the United States in 1951, later opening Vinifera Wine Cellars and forever changing the face of American wine.
Photograph courtesy of Dr. Konstantin Frank Vinifera Wine Cellars

Bottom Left: The new tasting pavilion accommodates the large number of visitors, all eager to try new blends and old vintages.

Facing Page: Chateau Frank's sparkling wine goes through procedures similar to the traditional varieties, including racking.

served the company as a successful hub to spread the word of Finger Lakes wine. Its proximity to Northeastern cities puts it in reach of a great number of people, drawing over 70,000 visitors each year. The winery thrives on its good name, relying heavily on word-of-mouth. Loyal fans act as Dr. Frank ambassadors, extending the quality reputation both nationally and globally.

Open every day of the week, the tasting room is surrounded by sweeping views of Keuka Lake and the winery grounds. Tasters can sample an array of wines, with varietals like Dr. Frank's Dry Riesling from the Keuka Lake vineyard. Particularly expressive of the region, this green-gold-hued selection has picked up the flavor of the slate-rich, New York soil. Critics often rave that this gives a crisp mineral character to the wine. The tasting room is open year-round, providing free wine samples to guests and greeting them with friendly, professional guides.

A virtual archive of awards attests to the hard work and success of Dr. Frank's team. Among others, Dr. Frank's low-yield, high-quality riesling has caught the nation's eye. Out of an impressive 4,000 entrants, Dr. Frank took home top honors in the Los Angeles International Wine Competition. Blends and vintages are gaining more accolades for the vineyard each year and have received publication appearances in *The Wall Street Journal, Food & Wine* and *The New York Times*. The winery received the Winery of the Year award from the New York Wine Classic in 2006 and the Best of the East award from the International Eastern Wine Competition.

Above Left: Rkatsiteli, ready for harvest in the fall, usually October, offers the wine a fruity complexity.

Above Right: The award-winning Dry Riesling possesses a crisp acidity, a pronounced mineral character and layers of mango, citrus and pear blossoms in the nose.

Facing Page: The land of Upstate New York brought Konstantin Frank's philosophies to life. After 300 years of resistance to European vines, Dr. Frank realized that the cold climate was not the problem. In fact, the region enhanced the grapes' flavors and proved nurturing to Vitis vinifera.

Even with all of the recognition and acknowledgement, Frederick gets his greatest kicks from hearing stories of life-long Dr. Frank aficionados. Wine drinkers who visited the property years ago return and endearingly recall detailed interactions with Konstantin. The current generation hopes to leave the same lasting impression, enriching the lives of people around the world through their love of winemaking. With the fourth generation poised to take the vineyard's reigns, Frederick sees a bright future for Dr. Frank's vision.

2007
DRY
RIESLING

FINGER LAKES

ALCOHOL 12% BY VOLUME

Wine & Fare

Dr. Frank Dry Riesling
Pair with grilled shrimp and lemon pepper seafood.

Dr. Frank Rkatsiteli
Pair with shellfish paella and spicy Thai dishes.

Dr. Frank Gewürztraminer
*Bold enough for Indian curries and marinated
pork tenderloins.*

Chateau Frank Blanc de Blancs
Pair with smoked salmon, peel-and-eat shrimp and sushi.

Tastings
Open to the public daily, year-round

Fox Run Vineyards

Penn Yan

In a story that echoes the hard-working pioneer spirit of the Northeast, Scott Osborn purchased Fox Run Vineyards in 1993 with hopes of transforming a struggling business. "When I bought Fox Run," he states candidly, "it was a modest operation with a middling reputation. I set out to change all that."

Scott quickly assembled a team of highly qualified specialists, now comprised of vineyard manager John Kaiser, comptroller Ruth Osborn, winemaker Peter Bell, and tasting room manager Dan Mitchell. Michael Lally joined as co-owner in 2006. Not just co-workers, this close-knit group enjoys a working environment fostered by Scott's philosophy that the pleasure of wine should be found not only in its consumption, but also in its production.

Located on a former dairy farm that dates from the Civil War era, Fox Run had been planted with its first grapes in 1984. In the early 1990s, wine was still being made in the refurbished dairy barn, but by mid-decade a state-of-the-art production facility had been built to accommodate the growing winery's need for more space. This left the beautiful, rustic barn available for tastings and elegant dinner parties.

Scott's links to the wine industry are long and varied, as he recalls his days as a bottle-labeler in a California wine company. He quickly added winemaking duties to his résumé and then took a job as a distributor, then general manager, for a large Long Island winery. Upon acquiring Fox Run, Scott and his wife Ruth moved into the property's elegantly restored farmhouse, though the country-gentleman lifestyle remains an elusive goal. "I am always at work," says Scott.

Top Left: Scott and Ruth Osborn—with Mya by their side—lead the winery's talented team.

Bottom Left: Empty and eager, picking bins wait for the harvest.

Facing Page: The sunrise at Fox Run Vineyards is enough to make any visitor consider an extended stay.

Fifty acres of the 110-acre property are planted with grapes, all of them the European vinifera species that are associated with the finest wines. The vineyards offer a stunning view of Seneca Lake, one that Peter maintains changes by the hour as the sun tracks across the sky. At least three soil types on the property allow for some distinct expressions of terroir. John Kaiser elaborates, "One of our vineyard blocks is actually planted on an ancient river delta, dating from when Seneca Lake was about twice its present size. Grapes from its sandy, loamy soil have a beautiful distinct flavor. It is fascinating."

An innovative trellis system was adopted in the mid-1990s, giving the grapes—which include chardonnay, riesling, gewürztraminer, cabernet franc and pinot noir—abundant exposure to the summer sun and cooling breezes. Perfectly ripe grapes make Peter's job much easier. "We make the best wines when our task in the winery is just to guide the fruit along and let the natural flavors express themselves," he adds modestly. In fact, the winemaker's job is continually challenging and humbling, and there is nothing hands-off about it.

A large tasting room accommodates the throngs of visitors the winery sees during the busy May to October tourist season. The winery actually had to rip out some beautiful old chardonnay vines to enlarge the

Top Left: The original winery location now houses the Fox Run Café and tasting room.

Middle Left: The bottling line reveals an industrial side of winemaking, efficient and mechanized.

Bottom Left: Winemaker Peter Bell, Nancy Irelan, Tricia Renshaw and Peter Howe stand in the production facility.

Facing Page: A European variety grown primarily in the Finger Lakes and Washington State, Lemberger grapes look as good on the vine as they taste in the bottle.

parking lot, as Scott wistfully remembers—he happens to have a special fondness for chardonnay in its elegant cool-climate manifestation. Fox Run offers tastings and tours seven days a week year-round. Visitors clearly enjoy their time with the friendly, approachable and knowledgeable staff, who tend to be big fans of Fox Run wines themselves.

Tours are free and run on the hour, typically lasting about 30 minutes. Visitors can also opt for a private VIP tour hosted by Scott, Peter or assistant winemaker Tricia. This allows guests an in-depth look at the vineyards and winery, culminating in a tasting of young wines from the barrel and bottlings not available in the tasting room. The VIP tour has been a great success with honeymooners, business executives and visitors from other countries, whose effusive letters and emails rave about the experience.

Fox Run's café offers up fuss-free gourmet fare, best enjoyed with a glass of wine of course. Executive chef Frank Caravita, a Culinary Institute of America alumnus, delivers tasty lunch items, and struts his stuff at dinner parties hosted by the winery. Wedding rehearsals, winemaker's dinners and intimate meals among friends keep him and his staff busy all year, with an emphasis on food prepared from fresh, local ingredients. On the first weekend in August, the winery hosts its annual Glorious Garlic Festival, featuring vendors, cooking demonstrations, live music and, yes, plenty of garlic.

Above Left: Warm and welcoming, sunlight streams into the gift shop throughout the day.

Above Right: Simple, delicious cuisine makes the menu at the Fox Run Café—an opportune spot to try out wine pairing skills.

Facing Page: With a spectacular view of Seneca Lake from the café, visitors get an appreciation for the region.

Fox Run has basked in a steady stream of positive press coverage from the beginning, with reviews in *Wine Spectator, Gourmet,* and *Wine & Spirits Magazine* among many others. Red wines, especially cabernet franc, pinot noir and a rich Meritage blend, tend to wow professionals and enthusiasts alike with their balance and approachability, but the best reviews of all have been for Fox Run's startling rieslings, made in both dry and off-dry styles. The winery's riesling was awarded a gold medal at the Riesling du Monde Competition in France—the only North American wine so honored. Scott recalls they "were grinning about that for weeks."

FOX RUN

VINEYARDS™

Reserve
Chardonnay

FINGER LAKES

2006

Produced and bottled by Fox Run Vineyards Inc.,
Penn Yan, N.Y. 14527 • 750 ml • Alc.12%/Vol. • Contains Sulfites

Wine & Fare

Reserve Chardonnay

Pair with corn chowder; roast duck with olives; frittatas and soufflés; fresh salad greens dressed with walnut oil; slow-roasted ribeye steak topped with Béarnaise sauce; artichokes with lemony Hollandaise sauce; and succulent lobster and scallops.

Riesling

Pair with all manner of spicy Szechuan foods, especially hot and sour soup; sweet and spicy spare ribs; smoked salmon; onion tart; Parma ham with figs; and poached peaches or pears.

Dry Riesling

Pair with Thai beef salad; sushi; gingery pot stickers; scallops; cold-roast pork; and bruschetta topped with green olives, sun dried tomatoes and shaved Parmesan.

Lemberger

Pair with pepper steak, slow-roasted vegetables with rosemary, spaghetti Bolognese, pork tenderloin, sausage dishes, empanadas, barbecued meats and antipasti.

Tastings
Open to the public daily, year-round

Glenora Wine Cellars

Dundee

What is the best way to spend a vacation? In a countryside inn? Sampling chef-prepared fare? Or touring a landmark winery? How about all of this? Glenora Wine Cellars offers visitors a range of opportunities to enjoy themselves, welcoming upward of 75,000 guests each year.

Glenora begins with the strong foresight of New York entrepreneurs. Gene Pierce, Edward Dalrymple, Eastman Beers and Howard Kimble jumped at a chance to start up a Finger Lakes winery on Seneca's shores. The opportunity arose with the Farm Winery Act of 1976, allowing vintners to run prosperous businesses with farm wineries. By 1977, the group had the establishment up and running, garnering instant praise and awards for the first vintage, including a handful of medals from the New York State Fair wine competition. And the winery has never looked back: Glenora pulled in 75 medals in a 12-month stretch and eventually went on to achieve the recognition of *Wine Spectator*, naming it as one of the world's best wineries. In 30 years, the winery has not stopped growing, producing 50,000 cases annually and reaching further than its founders had hoped.

Top Left: Gene Pierce is president and one of the four founding partners. Glenora Wine Cellars was the first winery on Seneca Lake, incorporated January 17, 1977.

Middle Left: Glenora Wine Cellars' Finger Lakes Chardonnay is must-try for tasting room visitors. The portfolio also includes a variety of wines, best known for riesling, pinot blanc, brut, syrah and port.
Photograph by Kristian S. Reynolds

Bottom Left: Winemaker Steve DiFrancesco has presided in his role for more than 15 years. Steve is highly regarded by his peers and has consistently produced award-winning wines.

Facing Page: The retail shop hosts 75,000 visitors annually, offering a spacious tasting room with spectacular views of the vineyards and Seneca Lake.
Photograph by Kristian S. Reynolds

Now, the operation is run by one of its originators, Gene Pierce, and his longtime friend Scott Welliver. After meeting at a sailboat race, the pair realized they had more in common than just nautical leisure. Shared visions between the two, The Inn at Glenora and Veraisons Restaurant have expanded the experience of visiting the winery. Now, visitors have a chance to stay awhile and relax at the inn, enjoying everything that Glenora has to offer.

With a variety of accommodations, 30 rooms are available on Glenora's lakeside land. Everything is at the guests' reach: southwestern views of Seneca Lake, vineyards and rolling hillsides; quiet mornings on a private balcony; fresh-brewed Starbucks coffee; the freshest cuisine; and of course, Glenora's wine. Stickley décor, plump pillow-top mattresses, inviting Jacuzzis and fireplaces add luxury to the rooms. Visitors choose from the Vintners Guestrooms, Deluxe Guestrooms or Select Guestrooms, all open and warm.

Veraisons Restaurant maintains a top-notch menu. Incorporating the freshest produce from local growers and farmers, the menu reflects the agriculture of the Finger Lakes through well prepared, innovative dishes. Open for breakfast, lunch and dinner, the restaurant has options like wild mushroom and spinach ravioli with feta cheese, ramps and brown-butter sage sauce; or Prince Edward Island mussels,

Top Right: Offering the entire portfolio of wines to taste and purchase, the retail shop remains open 364 days a year for tastings, guided cellar tours and retail sales.
Photograph by Kristian S. Reynolds

Bottom Right: Food and wine are the foremost concerns at Glenora Wine Cellars. Nothing compares to the experience of the perfect wine and food pairing.

Facing Page: The Inn at Glenora Wine Cellars and Veraisons Restaurant has an adjacent patio offering the perfect place to relax and enjoy a glass of wine upon arrival.

Previous Pages: The Inn at Glenora Wine Cellars offers 30 elegantly appointed rooms, all with a view of the vineyard and Seneca Lake.
Photograph by John Francis McCarthy

shrimp, fava beans and cilantro tossed in capellini pasta with a red curry cream sauce. Menus happily accommodate the occasion, from rehearsal dinners to company banquets to birthday celebrations. The setting varies as well, giving diners the option of alfresco meals or indoor seating. The restaurant features dramatic cathedral ceilings, large windows with remarkable views and a stone fireplace.

Glenora's wine list has an option for every palate. Selections include: Alpine White, a Cayuga and chardonnay blend; Cabernet Sauvignon; Bobsled Red, with hints of blackberry jam; Classic Blush; Dry Riesling; Gewürztraminer; and Port. Barrel Fermented Pinot Blanc is a dry white wine that has become a favorite among both the Glenora staff and visitors. Elegant and poised, the delicate pear and citrus flavors complement the soft oak and vanilla bouquet with a full lingering fresh fruit. Even wine cynics will be impressed.

In order to enjoy Glenora's lengthy list of wines, the calendar is filled with events that keep the community entertained. Festivities like Leaves and Lobsters on the Lawn ring in autumn with live music and unbeatable sights of Seneca Lake. Next to the wine, finger-licking fare takes center stage; a traditional

Top Left: Every guestroom at The Inn at Glenora Wine Cellars offers visitors the opportunity to take in the view from a private deck or patio. Quiet, tranquil and relaxing—guests never want to leave.
Photograph by Kristian S. Reynolds

Middle Left: Spacious, well appointed guestrooms include a complimentary bottle of wine, champagne upon arrival and a glass of port as a night cap.
Photograph by Kristian S. Reynolds

Bottom Left: Accommodation upgrades include rooms with a pillow-top king size bed, whirlpool tub and fireplace. Also available to guests on the Glenora campus is a two-bedroom guest house, nestled in the vineyard overlooking a pond. The accommodation has a full-size kitchen, living room, dining room, one and a half bathrooms and a spectacular sunroom.

Facing Page: Glenora Wine Cellars' 40-acre campus is breathtakingly beautiful from every vantage point. The grounds are immaculate, lush and green in the summer; and colorful and crisp in the fall. The property is welcoming to guests inside and out.
Photograph by Kristian S. Reynolds

Eastern lobster bake serves up steamed clams, local salt potatoes, Black Angus burgers and whole Maine lobsters. Other events include Jazz Greats at Glenora, Fine Art & Fine Wine and Ladies Night Out. True Glenora fans can join the Forbidden Fruit Wine Club.

The best way to experience Glenora Wine Cellars is to visit, and see the efforts of a group of visionaries. Take a break, relax and unwind in the beauty of Finger Lakes wine country.

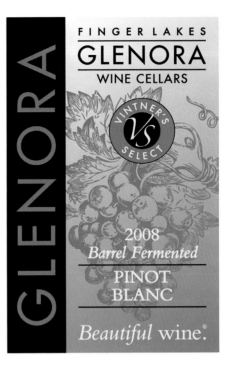

Wine & Fare

Barrel Fermented Pinot Blanc—Finger Lakes
*A perfect summer wine, pair with mild white fish,
light poultry and spicy shrimp dishes.*

Gewürztraminer
*Dry, with a clean, lingering finish, this bright
and flavorful wine is a great match for intense, savory entrées.*

Glenora Port
*Pair with vanilla bean crème brûlée, fresh raspberries
or enjoy alone as a night cap.*

Tastings
Open to the public daily, year-round

Goose Watch Winery

Romulus

I f history had a flavor, what would it taste like? How would century-old recipes for food and wine taste? Although it seems impossible to capture that essence, Goose Watch Winery in Romulus is doing just that. Among other varieties, the vineyards grow nearly extinct grapes that were popular over a hundred years ago—giving tasters the true flavor of a bygone era. These wines are difficult to find and offer visitors the most delicious history lesson they could imagine.

The winery's turn toward producing distinct beverages was decided when friends of the now-owners, the Petersons, held acreage on the western slopes of Cayuga Lake. It had come time to sell the land but the couple was frightened due to looming investors' incentives and housing expansion. Knowing they would preserve the land and take advantage of its agricultural potential, Dick and Cindy Peterson were the perfect buyers. They had already established one area winery, Swedish Hill; another seemed like a good idea. Transforming the property from chestnut groves with an aquaculture trout farm into vineyards with a burgeoning winery has happily satisfied both parties. While its former farmers left the land, the flourishing chestnuts have remained and are the honorary guest for autumn's Chestnut Festival.

Timing of the offer was spot-on for the Petersons, as they had been developing some new and rarer varieties of wine at Swedish Hill. Since son and owner Dave Peterson enjoyed visiting wineries that specialized in less run-of-the-mill varieties, the idea of dedicating an entire facility to the virtues of regionally scarce grapes was met in unanimous agreement. Goose Watch now produces Diamond, Rosé of Isabella and a premium cream sherry,

Top Left: The Goose Watch tasting room is located on Cayuga Lake, welcoming visitors year-round to its idyllic and beautiful setting.

Bottom Left: Fall is one of the most popular seasons to visit the winery. Visitors can enjoy a stroll through the vineyards while the grapes ripen on the vines adjacent to the tasting room—where guests fully experience the true character of the wines.

Facing Page: Vineyards at Goose Watch thrive on high limestone soils, grown on the shores of Cayuga Lake. The terrain is ideal for production of many of the winery's hard-to-grow and hard-to-find varietals such as viognier, villard blanc and lemberger.

bottling the flavor of Finger Lakes history. The Diamond variety has achieved a virtually unheard of status for a wine made from native American grapes, winning the Sweepstakes Award in the Best of Show White Wine category at the Riverside International Wine Competition in California. Striking a chord with today's connoisseurs just as they did more than a century ago, these wines give tasters a sip of the 1800s.

Melody and traminette—newer white wine grapes developed by Cornell University—are two more difficult finds that also appear here. Goose Watch's Melody is a crisp, semi-dry wine that offers delicate floral and vanilla aromas with bright, citrus-like flavors that complement poultry dishes—with the exception of wild goose, of course. The Traminette won a stunning six awards in 2007 with four of them earning gold, adding to the 20-some gold medals the winery rakes in each year. No palate left behind, additional varietals include pinot grigio, viognier, lemberger and cabernet sauvignon, all receiving widespread acclaim. Travelers stopping in the mountainside town of Lake Placid can also sample a full line-up of the winery's flavors. Quaint, cozy and full of charm, the downtown Alpine Mall offers bottles for tasting and purchase.

Top Right: Rustic yet elegant, the tasting room includes oak floors, bars and trim harvested from the farm. An extensive range of gift items includes everything from wine related accessories to gourmet food items to logo shirts.

Bottom Right: The tasting room has two upstairs sampling areas as well as the tasting room on the main floor. Visitors can enjoy a view of the downstairs from the balcony, connecting the two upstairs rooms.

Facing Page Top: One of the large ponds on the winery property features a large stainless steel goose perched above the pond, watching over the property.

Facing Page Bottom Left: Owners Dick, Cindy and Dave Peterson opened Goose Watch in 1997 and have positioned the family-owned and operated winery as one of the most respected, as well as most unique, properties in the region.

Facing Page Bottom Right: The Goose Watch product line stands out and offers a diverse selection, featuring varietal wines such as Lemberger, Pinot Grigio, Traminette, dessert wines such as Finalé White Port and Classic Cream Sherry, as well as sparkling wines and fun and fruity blends.

A true enophile and always ready for a vintner's challenge, Dave particularly enjoys creating wines from grapes with a hard-to-grow reputation. He and his team now know the 120-acre parcel so well—from the lake's slopes to the fertile fields further uphill—that no growing option seems impossible. This particular terroir offers a complexity to the wine, giving all the varieties a flavorful hint of the earth's high limestone content.

The atmosphere of the winery matches its characteristic wines, with a restored barn from the 19th century as the tasting room. Milled from site-grown trees, rich oak floors and oak bars adorn the spacious, rustic interior. The room is put to good use during its festivals, like the annual summer Strawberry Festival. This festival warrants a delicious blending of two selections, Spumante Champagne and Strawberry Splendor, to create a Goose Watch original—a perfect accompaniment

to strawberry desserts. Mild summers lend themselves to picnicking on the winery's designated grounds or the relaxed deck. With access by boat via Cayuga Lake, Goose Watch Winery is a perfect destination for a full day of the region's beauty.

So, why the name Goose Watch? While looking at the land before purchase, the Petersons noticed some regular visitors on the property: geese—specifically Canadian and Snow Geese. The family

Above: The picturesque Goose Watch property features chestnut groves, vineyards and a panoramic view of Cayuga Lake.
Photograph courtesy of Goose Watch

Facing Page: Winery grounds are perfect for picnics, whether the basket is packed with home grown favorites or fresh items from the tasting room.

found a stainless-steel, radio-tower-mounted goose watching over the property's large pond, a clear indication of the previous owner's homage. As a thankful gesture for the borrowed land they were sitting on, the Petersons extended the homage and used the native resident as a namesake, opening Goose Watch Winery in 1997. The stand-out name has brought together the unlikely pairing of geese and grapes—quite successfully—giving a fitting title to one of the region's most distinctive wineries.

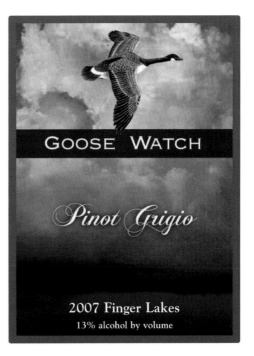

Wine & Fare

Pinot Grigio
Accompanies pasta with garlic and olive oil or broiled scallops.

Traminette
Pair with oysters, smoked trout or salmon—Asian or Cajun dishes, as well.

Chambourcin
Pair with venison entrées, pasta with red sauce or turkey.

Tastings
Open to the public year-round

Hermann J. Wiemer Vineyard

Dundee

Riesling-obsessed connoisseurs know how important Hermann J. Wiemer is to wine. His pioneering work in the New York Finger Lakes has developed a loyal following over the years, beginning his self-named winery in 1973. His fans know that there is no better candidate to set the Riesling standard; his life story seems custom-made for a foremost expert on Vitis vinifera.

Born to enophiles, Hermann grew up in a wine-laden world. His mother's family had dedicated more than 300 years to the trade. In Bernkastel, Germany, Hermann's father directed the restoration of Mosel Valley vineyards after World War II had taken its toll. Mosel Valley is known for its continental climate, arduous vineyards and superior riesling grapes. As the head of the Agricultural Experimentation Station, Hermann's father pioneered the technique of grafting American rootstock with Mosel vinifera to help the vines thrive. Hermann studied hand grafting and attended Germany's premier winemaking and viticultural institutions before leaving for the United States to establish Hermann J. Wiemer Vineyard on the shores of Seneca Lake. Here, the well drained sloping shale-stone bedrock and Honeoye silt loam soil lends itself to the production of what critics consider to be some of the most developed and distinct German-style wines.

Top Left: Potted nursery vines are available for sale at the winery.

Bottom Left: The lineup of the estate-grown wines continues to impress visitors.

Facing Page: The vineyards sit with a beautiful backdrop of Seneca Lake.

The German theme continues in the style of the solid winery, creating an attraction all on its own. Designed after the German Museum of Architecture, the winery is sleek, modern and undoubtedly a work of art. The scissor-trussed barn is more than 90 years old and exhibits stark, striking walls behind stainless steel tanks. Straight lines and modern elegance interacts with traditional winemaking to make Hermann J. Wiemer Vineyard a one-off experience. In this remarkable space, single-vineyard bottlings are processed and cared for, developing the strong and true character of the grapes.

A nursery sits on the property as well, where Hermann honed his grafting skills on American soil. Attracting everyone from do-it-yourself types to viticultural scholars, the nursery was established due to a lack of commercial plant sales in the 1970s. It remains one of the highlights of visiting the winery today.

The elegance of German viticulture has been passed on to Hermann's long-term winemaker Fred Merwarth and estate manager Oskar Bynke. They spend countless hours perfecting the legacy that distinguishes Hermann J. Wiemer Vineyard. Drawing on Hermann as their advisor and mentor, the new team continues to focus on terroir-driven wines—at Hermann J. Wiemer Vineyard, wines have the authentic varietal character and balance that differentiates them from other wines.

Above Left: Surrounded with a classic stone wall, the 90-year old scissor-trussed barn with a fully working winery inside and aging facility for sparkling wines remains a key piece of the winery's history.
Photograph by Maressa Merwarth

Above Right: Designed by an award-winning team of Cornell architects, the building encloses a unique white cathedral-like interior that counterpoints the bare wooden walls and sleek Italian stainless steel tanks.
Photograph by Maressa Merwarth

Facing Page: The view at the winery rivals the vineyards in Mosel Valley.
Photograph by Maressa Merwarth

Enormous effort goes into crafting small batches of the demanding wines—pinot noir, gewürztraminer, blanc de blanc and cabernet franc and five rieslings. The work pays off in the defined, sought-after flavors. Wiemer Vineyard wines are estate bottled and grown, exemplifying the ethos of Hermann J. Wiemer Vineyard: quality.

At the winery visitors receive a warm, personalized welcome, and taste wine in a graceful room staffed with highly knowledgeable personnel. Hermann J. Wiemer Vineyard has led the way in creating visibility for the region, as its wines receive excellent ratings when tasted alongside the best of their kind from elsewhere in the world.

Hermann J. Wiemer
VINEYARD

Wines in the finest European tradition, from the heart of the Finger Lakes

WINE & FARE

Hermann J. Wiemer Blanc De Noir
Pair with tuna tartar alongside roasted beets and picked cucumbers.

Hermann J. Wiemer Dry Riesling
Accompanies chorizo with caramelized firefly hakurei turnips.

Hermann J. Wiemer Dry Gewürztraminer
Pair with curried shrimp on cumin-scented basmati rice.

Hermann J. Wiemer Select Late Harvest
Pair with ice cream atop meringue nests and sauced with fresh raspberries, strawberries and blueberries in Grand Marnier.

Tastings
Open to the public daily, seasonally

Heron Hill Vineyards

Hammondsport

Heron Hill Winery is a standout destination. With a prime location on the west side of Keuka Lake, the awe-inspiring winery features modern architecture and breathtaking views of the surrounding mountains. The winery was originally built in 1977, and a complete overhaul was concluded in 2001 that resulted in a composition of three distinct architectural themes. Representative of surrounding farm silos, a tower rises in the center of the building while a structure over the café patio reflects the Greek Revival period—common among the area's older homes. Appropriately styled after an oversized wine barrel, the vaulted grand tasting room mimics the unique experience of actually being inside the cask.

The wine cellar sits under the main facility with three of the four sides below ground, providing excellent year-round temperature control in an environment conducive to high-quality wine. Not to be outdone by the luxurious aboveground facility, the Heron Hill cellar is outfitted with the most advanced winemaking equipment. Optimum production amounts to about 27,000 cases per year.

During the late 1960s, John and Josephine met at the University of Denver. The sun was shining, their hearts were fluttering and the wine was flowing, albeit Ripple red and white. From that glorious day onward, John and Josephine have enjoyed life and love—and wine.

By the time John graduated with the intent to teach English, he was reading organic gardening magazines and had been bitten by the "back to the earth" bug. After marrying, John and Josephine searched for their promised land considering Washington, Oregon

Top Left: The selection of specialty dessert wines are crafted by winemaker Thomas Laszlo.

Bottom Left: Seasonal vineyard colors make autumn an unmistakable time of year.

Facing Page: Heron Hill Winery sits perched above Keuka Lake.

and British Columbia; but the two stargazers landed in John's backyard—Seneca Point, Naples, New York. There they lived the simple life, devotedly helping their neighbors with the grape harvest. Something about chasing a wagon down a vineyard row with a 40-pound box of hand-picked grapes struck the two budding enophiles as the good life.

Spring of 1972 saw the Ingles plant 20 acres of grapes including chardonnay, riesling, cabernet franc and pinot noir. They cleared the land and planted some 12,000 vines.

By planting European Vitis vinifera varieties, the Ingles were part of a small group of pioneers that bucked the tried-and-true trend of growing native varieties and French-American hybrids. Fortunately, the Ingle Vineyard located on Canandaigua Lake proved to be a top site for the production of high quality, distinct wines. The soils are naturally well-drained and the mix of gravel, shale and loam located on south-sloping hills fit the classic model of what a grand cru vineyard should possess.

The 15-acre vineyard surrounding Heron Hill is composed mainly of riesling with smaller amounts of chardonnay and white muscat. These varieties were planted in 1968, making it one of the oldest riesling vineyards in North America. It is a slightly cooler site than Ingle Vineyard, with shallow slate and shale soils that produce mineral-driven wines that take years to blossom, rivaling the great rieslings produced in Germany, Alsace and Austria.

Top Right: The original Ingle Vineyard homestead reveals the winery's growth over the last 40 years.

Bottom Right: The Ingle Farm root cellar gives a peek into the winery's humble beginning.

Facing Page: Inside the vaulted tasting hall, guests can sample an array of Heron Hill wines.

Heron Hill has been making wines of distinction from both vineyard sites for more than 30 years with the main emphasis on riesling. Producing over nine styles from bone dry and semi-sweet, all the way up to decadent, ultra premium Late Harvest and Icewine, Heron Hill is on the leading edge of riesling production in North America. With the addition of winemaker Thomas Laszlo in 2002, the dedication to this top-notch product has propelled Heron Hill Winery to the forefront of cool climate wine production.

Canadian born with Hungarian parents, Thomas graduated from the prestigious University of Guelph with a degree in farm management. While his training in agriculture was of great assistance, Thomas' winemaking skills came while working at Henry of Pelham Family Estate Winery. After several years as assistant winemaker, Thomas and his wife Jane made a radical move to the Tokaj region of Hungary, an area known as the world's foremost producer of noble sweet wines. These fabled wines were the toast of European aristocracy from the

17th to 19th centuries, enjoyed by the likes of King Louis the XIV, Peter the Great, Voltaire and the papacy.

After turbulent wars and Soviet occupation, the wines of Tokaj faded into obscurity. With the Wall down in 1989, new investments were flowing into Tokaj with the hopes of restoring the region. After achieving remarkable success, Thomas and his wife Jane had a baby girl and returned to North America. During his travels throughout Europe, Thomas was able to pursue his passion for riesling and spent considerable time exchanging winemaking techniques with top producers.

Above Left: The winery building features aspects of Greek Revival architecture that is typical of many of the 19th-century homes in western New York.

Above Right: An entrance ramp leads visitors toward the observation tower, offering beautiful panoramic views.

Facing Page: Riesling vines are often shrouded in fog due to the high level of moisture from the lakes.

Executive Producer: ERNESTO ALCALDE
Co-Executive Producer: DAVID WECHSLER

05/13/10 Draft
Film

Producer: FRANCESCA BUCCELLATO
Director: ERNESTO ALCALDE

THE GARBAGE COLLECTOR

Written by
DAVID WECHSLER

KLR Productions, Inc
VANMAAR PICTURES
1220 Lindstrom Dr
New York NY 10011

Thomas' decision to accept winemaking responsibilities at Heron Hill was an obvious choice. The culmination of his efforts has resulted in an explosion of accolades for the winery. Most notably, Heron Hill Winery's 2002 Ingle Vineyard Riesling won the Best in Show White Wine in the prestigious 2004 San Francisco International Wine Competition, chosen from upward of 2,000 entries.

More recently, Heron Hill was selected as the only East Coast winery featured in the pilot segment of the documentary series "Jancis Robinson's Wines of America." With this recognition Heron Hill emerges as a beacon for the future of Finger Lakes riesling and fine wine production.

HERON HILL
WINERY

WINE & FARE

Eclipse
(33% merlot, 34% cabernet franc, 33% cabernet sauvignon)
Pair with venison or beef and thyme stew.

Semi-Sweet Riesling
(100% riesling)
Pair with avocado, orange and flank-steak salad.

Semi-Dry Riesling
(100% riesling)
Pair with cabbage leaves stuffed with ground sirloin and rice.

Ingle Vineyard Unoaked Chardonnay
(100% chardonnay)
Pair with smoked salmon with dill cream cheese.

Tastings
Open to the public daily, year-round

Hunt Country Vineyards

Branchport

At the Hunts' Thanksgiving dinner table, warmth and chatter fill the air. Art steals away to check the forecast and discovers a sharp cold front advancing from Canada. The excited call goes out to cousins and friends and winter clothes are dragged out. Preparations are underway for Hunt Country Vineyards' harvest of Vidal Blanc, their prized grape for ice wine.

At four a.m., a frosty thermometer on the porch reads 12 degrees—perfect. By dawn, the picking crew is fortified with breakfast and a tractor takes them out to the vineyards; Gus, the Bernese mountain dog, is happy to be going along. The crew proceeds down the vineyard rows, picking the frozen grapes, hard as stones, and putting them into baskets. Hours later they will load dozens of full picking boxes onto a wagon for the trip back to the winery where the grapes will be pressed frozen. Ice crystals, skins and seeds will remain in the press, and out will trickle the tiniest stream of intensely sweet and flavorful nectar. After months of careful fermentation, the sweetness, alcohol and acidity will be perfectly balanced in a wine rich with honey and subtle tropical fruit flavors. A beautiful new vintage of Vidal Blanc Ice Wine will be bottled in the spring.

Art's great-great-grandparents Ambrose and Caroline Beers Hunt purchased the core of the present-day Hunt farm in 1852. Art Hunt and Joyce Haines grew up in Corning, New York, married in 1971 and fell in love with the 170-acre farm, high on the sloping western flank of Keuka Lake, then under the management of an elderly uncle of Art's. In 1973 they moved to the farm and planted 60 acres of grapes. Merger activity within the wine industry soon forced grape prices down below most growers' cost, and although they considered it a long shot, Art and Joyce threw themselves into establishing a winery.

Top Left: For Caroline, Jonathan, Joyce and Art Hunt, winemaking is a deep-rooted family tradition. Winery dogs Mouse, Molly and Gus have the best backyard around.

Bottom Left: Countless awards have been bestowed upon Hunt Country's wines.

Facing Page: The vineyards provide a lovely backdrop for Hunt Country Vineyards.
Photograph by John Francis McCarthy

In 1981 they released their first vintages, "seven modest whites and a modest red," as Art puts it. To their stunned delight, all won statewide awards. They began traveling regularly the 300 miles to New York City to sell their wines at a weekend farmers' market, and people took notice: An influential pastry chef selected Hunt Country's Vidal Blanc Ice Wine for a United Nations gala dinner—it was a hit.

The Hunts have since built a modern warehouse and expanded their tiny tasting room into a beautiful, airy building. Their wine portfolio has grown to include classic vinifera varietals and several distinctive wines like their Jefferson Cup-winning Vignoles. Cool September nights on Keuka Lake preserve the delicate fruit flavors that develop during the daytime; gravelly loam soil ensures excellent water drainage; and sloping vineyards provide excellent air movement, thereby preventing frosts.

The experience and passion of winemaker Christopher Wirth have translated the land's natural gifts into success for the winery. Chris spent 25 years in the wine industry in California and Oregon before returning to his native New York in early 2005. Hunt Country wines have amassed more than 60 prestigious awards since 2004. Joyce commented enthusiastically, "Chris brought his love for Pinot Gris from Oregon to us, and our first vintage ever won Best Pinot Gris in New York in 2007."

Art and Joyce's son Jonathan, and his wife Caroline, are the sixth generation of Hunts on the family farm.

Top Left: The Hunt family lives on-site and takes in majestic countryside views day and night.

Middle Left: Netting protects the delectable ice wine grapes.

Bottom Left: The tasting room's wood detailing and open layout invite guests to linger, enjoy themselves.

Facing Page: Autumn time in Branchport is nothing short of spectacular.

They express their abiding love for the farm in their stewardship of the land: Most of the by-products of winemaking are composted into fertilizer; weed-controlling groundcover plants are being researched; and tractors run on biodiesel. The two Hunt daughters, Carolyn and Suzanne, remain connected to the farm and offer ideas for sustainability and marketing.

Hunt Country welcomes more than 40,000 visitors a year, and the wonderful tasting room team encourages guests to relax, enjoy and learn during their stay. Art and his family are grateful that so many return again and again to share their passion for the Finger Lakes region and Hunt Country wines.

WINE & FARE

Hunt Country Meritage
Pair with rack of lamb, fine cuts of beef and creamy cheeses.

Hunt Country Pinot Gris
*Pair with smoked salmon, mild cheeses,
light poultry dishes and pasta.*

Hunt Country Semi-Dry Riesling
Pair with pork, veal, poultry and seafood, especially crab.

Hunt Country Vidal Blanc Ice Wine
*Pair with fruit or nut tarts and pies, cheesecake,
crème caramel and fine pâté.*

Tastings
Open to the public daily, year-round

Keuka Spring Vineyards

Penn Yan

What began as a family dream has evolved into a flourishing, successful business and a highly regarded winery in the Finger Lakes. In the early 1980s Len and Judy Wiltberger had the opportunity to purchase 30 acres of land overlooking beautiful Keuka Lake. With their love of wine and winemaking experience, they planted several grape varieties at the site. They opened a tasting room in the mid-1980s, adjacent to the vineyards, with 1985 being their first vintage.

Len and Judy are committed to making consistent, high-quality, award-winning wine, hand-crafted from vine to bottle. From the beginning, they have believed that Keuka Lake is an area capable of producing world-class wine. They also believe that each visitor to the tasting room should have the best wine tasting experience possible, enjoying fine wine and the company of a well-trained and hospitable staff, in an atmosphere that complements learning about and enjoying their wines. Today Len and Judy's daughter, Jeanne, manages promotion while their son Mark is part of the winemaking team.

Top Left: Founded in 1981 by Len and Judy Wiltberger, Keuka Spring Vineyards produces acclaimed Finger Lakes wines.

Middle Left: Visitors love the winery's scenic vistas.
Photograph by Jeanne Wiltberger

Bottom Left: Overlooking the east side of Keuka Lake, the tasting room features a stone terrace for picnics and tastings.
Photograph by Jeanne Wiltberger

Facing Page: The pergola invites guests into the tasting room.

Keuka Spring Vineyards lies on the east side of Keuka Lake, where the gentle west-facing slope retains the sun late into the evening, lengthening the growing season and providing an ideal microclimate for premium grapes. From these grapes, Len and Judy produce internationally recognized chardonnay, riesling, cabernet, merlot and gewürztraminer, as well as wines that highlight the unique fruit characteristics of the grapes of the region.

Above: Built in 2004, Keuka Spring's new building is adjacent to the vineyards.
Photograph by Len Wiltberger

Left: Len and Judy's son Mark supervises the winemaking while their daughter Jeanne manages promotion.

Facing Page: Premium wine grapes and superb winemaking yield the world-class wines for which Keuka Spring is known.
Photograph by Jeanne Wiltberger

Since its inception over the years, Keuka Spring has received numerous awards for quality. The cabernet franc earned the prestigious Governor's Cup, signifying the single best wine in New York State for that year. Other accolades include many Best in Class awards for various wines, double gold and gold medals, and rieslings as Governor's Cup finalists.

Surrounded by vineyards and commanding a gorgeous view of Keuka Lake, in the new winery and tasting room opened in 2004, visitors can enjoy world-class wine and be treated to the personal touch and tradition of hospitality for which Keuka Spring is known.

WINE & FARE

Riesling

Pair this off-dry wine with grilled chicken, salmon, crab, cream soups, Gouda or Cheddar cheese, Caesar salads or just about anything.

Gewürztraminer

Enjoy with chicken, shrimp, strong cheeses and Asian cuisine. The character of this wine is perfect with spicy—or any—food.

Cabernet Franc

Pair with roasted chicken, pork loin, turkey or sirloin steaks.

Miller's Cove Red
(merlot, cabernet sauvignon)

Versatile and full-bodied, this red pairs well with burgers, beef stew, rack of lamb or steak.

Tastings
Open to the public, seasonally

Named after the New York town lying on the eastern slopes of Cayuga Lake, King Ferry Winery has been producing some of the country's finest chardonnay since 1988. The longest in the Finger Lakes region, Cayuga Lake stretches nearly 40 miles with the winery's vineyard taking up 32 flavorful acres.

The small farm began when proprietors Pete and Tacie Saltonstall partnered up with friends in nearby Ithaca. Running a restaurant at the time, their friends introduced the idea of a winery—Pete and Tacie were sold. As an added bonus, the restaurant had an extensive cellar full of wonderful Burgundy wines. Pete had farmed for much of his life and had spent time in Napa Valley where his older brother developed hillside vineyards. Although their friends later left the trade, the Saltonstalls had found their calling. As winery business picked up, Pete's balancing act with his construction business became increasingly difficult. The pair agreed to forge ahead full-steam into the world of wine.

Pete's father purchased the Treleaven farm—hence the Treleaven brand name—where the Saltonstalls now run their operation. Many of the staff members have been with Pete and Tacie for years. Wholesale marketer Kim Shevalier and administrative assistant Leah Parker have been loyal to the company for over 18 years, a testament to the warm working environment. Slightly newer to the staff, Tacie's brother John Balliett, manages the vineyard and Lindsay Stevens has stepped in to help Pete as the winemaker.

Top Left: Owner Tacie Saltonstall and vineyard manager John Balliett often share a laugh.

Bottom Left: Baby grapes reach for the sun in early June.

Facing Page: Days full of blue skies and sunshine provide the best weather for seeing the winery.
Photograph by John Francis McCarthy

Gourmet cook, wine pairing expert and tasting room manager Chris Couch liked the Saltonstalls so much, he decided to legally become part of the family by marrying Courtney, Pete and Tacie's daughter. Along with Courtney, the other children, Hattie and Leverett have pitched in over the years in all phases of the business. Leverett's people skills became evident when he began conducting winery tours as a 10-year-old.

The family warmth at King Ferry beams from the entire staff, welcoming guests into an easy atmosphere. Since 1987, when the winery was built, the Saltonstalls have expanded their production space and tasting room to five times its original size to offer plenty of room to friends and family—old and new.

In the tradition of farming, the grapes are hand-tended and carefully selected to make 15 different wines, including the newest additions of vidal and vignoles. Growing on the lower level of the sloping acreage, pinot noir and cabernet franc fill the rows. Further up, the land offers gewürztraminer, riesling and chardonnay—the superstar of the Treleaven vineyards.

Top Right: The entrance to the tasting room features a hand-painted mural by owner Tacie Saltonstall.

Bottom Right: Murals on the interior reflect the surrounding countryside.

Facing Page: The vineyard offers a spectacular view of Cayuga Lake.

King Ferry Chardonnays are world class, with a wide range of flavor notes. The Main Chardonnay—Tacie's favorite—offers up an easy drinking, well-balanced chardonnay without too much oak. Buttery, with a smooth, rich mouthfeel, the Reserve is Burgundian in style. Aged in Polish, French and Hungarian oak barrels, the vinification process enhances the grape's quality. Instead of trying to compete with large producers, the Saltonstalls focus on crafting the perfect chardonnay in smaller quantities and creating a delicious niche for appreciative wine drinkers.

No longer the best kept secret, the Treleaven rieslings exhibit some wonderful floral and mineral characteristics. Treleaven's Semi-dry, Dry and Late Harvest Rieslings all carry the mineral essence of the land—one that wine judges clearly admire. The International Eastern Wine Competition awarded the Best Dry Riesling honor to the 2005 vintage; the riesling beat out competitiors from 12 countries, four provinces and 32 states.

Left: Award-winning Treleaven wines proudly display their medals above racks of Riesling.

Facing Page: Just as eye-catching as the vineyards, regional wild flowers add color to the land.

Committed to improving the image and stature of New York wines, Pete and Tacie Saltonstall have been a strong force behind changing New York laws, allowing for interstate shipment of wines, the high point of which was attending the review by the U.S. Supreme Court of the shipping case. As a chairman of the board at the New York Wine and Grape Foundation, Pete is not only invested in King Ferry Winery—with the devoted work of the entire family—but the future of the Finger Lakes.

Dry

Treleaven

Riesling

CAYUGA LAKE

Estate —••— Bottled

— *Produced & Bottled by* —

KING FERRY WINERY, INC. KING FERRY, N.Y. 13081
ALC. 10.9% BY VOL. • CONTAINS SULFITES

WINE & FARE

Treleaven Cabernet Franc

Pair with Thai food; blackened steak; pasta arrabiata; and chocolate-covered cherries and raspberries.

Treleaven Main Chardonnay

Pair with Parmesan black-peppercorn biscotti; orange and onion-stuffed roasted turkey; and chocolate-covered peanut butter bonbons.

Treleaven Semi-Dry Riesling

Pair with nearly anything, including a wide assortment of cheeses; Cajun-spiced pork loin with an orange-mustard Creole sauce; barbecue; and strawberry rhubarb pie.

Tastings
Open to the public daily, seasonally

Knapp Winery

Romulus

Approachable, simple and undoubtedly elegant, Knapp Winery and Vineyard Restaurant is an escape for any day of the week. Perfect for special occasions or a quick glass of wine with friends, the winery has a reputation for warm welcomes. The setting is ideal for relaxation and taking advantage of the natural beauty on Cayuga Lake.

Knapp's vineyards boast of chardonnay, cabernet sauvignon, riesling and merlot, plus hold the distinction as the first Finger Lakes' vineyard to grow cabernet sauvignon grapes for winemaking. Wine drinkers enjoy signature options like Prism, a light, classic Bordeaux blend or the Estate Dry Riesling with delicate hints of apricots and limes. Reserve Chardonnay, Cayuga White and Sangiovese make the Knapp wine list, as well. And fruit fans will love George's Peach, Knapp Loganberry and Black Cherry, fresh and crisp. Grappa—an earthy flavored, hand-crafted liquor—Limencello, Ruby Port and sparkling wine give visitors a chance to sample something unexpected.

Top Left: With beautifully landscaped grounds, the winery and restaurant is a 100-acre farm complete with a stocked pond—guests may even find chickens roaming around in the summertime.
Photograph by Kristian S. Reynolds

Middle Left: The landscape in Finger Lakes wine country is worth the trip to the area. Knapp Winery and Vineyard Restaurant offers good directional signs to assist guests in finding their way.

Bottom Left: Guests can enjoy a light snack or a hearty lunch inside or on the patio, whether under a trellis of vines or right next to the vineyards. There is nothing like a wine country meal in a wine country setting.
Photograph by Kristian S. Reynolds

Facing Page: Cayuga Lake is unforgettable. Every traveler should stop by, take a stroll through the grounds and soak in the view; it is a beautiful place.
Photograph by John Francis McCarthy

Over the years, Knapp has expanded its offerings to fit the demands of an ever-growing crowd. But it all began with Doug and Suzie Knapp, who bought the property in 1977. The couple began studying winemaking, honed their skills and learned exactly what the Finger Lakes had to offer. The first estate-grown vintage came out in 1982, met with success and accolades by the community. Just seven years later, a restaurant and retail shop opened, followed by the use of an alembic pot still, the first working commercial model in Finger Lakes Wine Country. Gene Pierce and Scott Welliver, also the owners of Glenora Wine Cellars, purchased the winery—still and all—in 2000 and have watched the company flourish ever since, growing to offer 30 wine varieties and six cordials, or brandies.

Knapp Vineyard Restaurant gives visitors a taste of the region. Lying on the Cayuga Lake Wine Trail, the eatery is a perfect resting spot to sample the flavor of the Finger Lakes. Menu items come in all sizes and shapes, from midday snacks like cheese and cracker boards to more filling meals like herbed onion, Gouda-topped Knapp burgers on kaiser rolls.

Top Left: From the moment they first step on to the property, guests fall in love with Knapp Winery and Vineyard Restaurant. The surroundings set the stage for a relaxing time with a significant other, a group of friends or family.
Photograph by John Francis McCarthy

Middle Left: Gene Pierce, president and owner, can often be found on a tractor or in the vineyards. His background in the farm industry has made Knapp a very special place.

Bottom Left: With over 25 years of producing high quality, estate wines, Knapp has a fan base that spans many generations. Whether for a special occasion or just a reason to get together, it is always a good time for a Knapp.
Photograph by Kristian S. Reynolds

Facing Page: Fifty acres of well-maintained vines produce the highest quality grapes for estate wines.
Photograph by John Francis McCarthy

The restaurant space also serves as a venue for special occasions and events, with no shortage of fantastic wine. Some guests find it difficult to leave the winery, which is why the Knapp lake house is almost never empty. Ideal for summer vacations or romantic getaways, the accommodations include a full kitchen, wraparound deck and views to write home about.

Riesling

FINGER LAKES

2 0 0 7

KNAPP

WINE & FARE

Merlot

Pair with creamy mushroom soup, a blend of portobello mushrooms, garlic, white onions, olive oil, heavy cream, Knapp Merlot and savory beef broth.

Estate Dry Riesling

Pair with herbed citrus seafood medley—a fresh mixture of calamari, scallops, shrimp, thyme, red and yellow peppers, olive oil and lemon juice.

Prism

Pair with Knapp Winery and Vineyard Restaurant's zucchini casserole, baked with farm-grown zucchini, ground spicy sausage, tomato paste, oregano, Vidalia onions, sharp Cheddar and Parmesan.

Tastings

Open to the public daily, year-round

Lamoreaux Landing Wine Cellars

Lodi

Never being at the mercy of others has its advantages, and Lamoreaux Landing Wine Cellars is just the place to prove it. Maintaining complete control over the quality of wine from their rolling vineyards to their award-winning winery, the crew at Lamoreaux produces some of the region's most notable wines.

Mark Wagner began the business in 1990, adding a winery to the vineyards his parents had bought more than 40 years earlier. The commercial operation began as a method of showcasing the European Vitis vinifera grapes that his family had learned to grow so well. As the years passed, the operation grew, accumulating vineyard acres, two winery additions and an arsenal of awards along the way—more than 550. Now, Lamoreaux Landing, named for the nearby steamboat dock used on Seneca Lake in the 1800s, meticulously manages more than 100 acres of vines, separated into more than 20 different vineyard blocks.

Spread across the eastern shores, the vineyards grow chardonnay, riesling, cabernet franc, gewürztraminer, pinot noir, merlot, cabernet sauvignon and vidal blanc. Rows and rows of vines benefit year-round from the moderating effects of Seneca Lake. Harsh winters can drop well below zero, making fragile vines vulnerable to the weather's whim.

Top Left: Owner Mark Wagner personally tastes each lot in the Lamoreaux Landing wine cellar.
Photograph by Kristian S. Reynolds

Bottom Left: With decades of viticultural experience, Mark Wagner founded Lamoreaux Landing when he produced his first wines from the 1990 vintage.
Photograph by Jon Reis / www.jonreis.com

Facing Page: Lamoreaux Landing's stunning Greek-Revival building was named as one of the most notable buildings built in New York during the 20th century by the American Institute of Architects.
Photograph by Kristian S. Reynolds

Radiant heat from the water insulates the vines and mitigates the damage of the subzero temperatures. In the summer, unique wind patterns, diverse soil types, and the perfect amount of sunlight result in an ideal equation—making this area of the state a perfect location for viticulture. Always looking toward the future, Lamoreaux Landing has placed a strong emphasis on sustainable initiatives, which preserve its ability to produce the highest quality fruit for generations to come. Sensitive to even the small details, Mark and his staff do their part to hold up green standards, meeting the ever-increasing awareness of environmental concerns.

Situated between the Old Passmore and Yellow Dog Vineyards, the winery sits high above sea level, providing memorable 25-mile views of the lake and

surrounding area: the best in the region. The building itself is a view in its own right. With a commanding presence and Greek Revival architecture, the building is just as enjoyable as the land it sits on. Designed by Ithaca-born Bruce Corson, the space plays host to events year-round. Lamoreaux also appears at a number of off-site events all over the Northeast.

Above: The winery view, as seen from the New Passmore Cabernet Franc Vineyard, is not to be missed.
Photograph by John Francis McCarthy

Right: The wine cellars welcome visitors who choose to travel along scenic Route 414 in Lodi.
Photograph courtesy of Lamoreaux Landing

Facing Page: Showcased on the gently sloping hills along Seneca Lake, the winery looks stunning from the Yellow Dog Vineyards.
Photograph courtesy of Lamoreaux Landing

Perpetually full, the winery offers something for everybody, which explains why demand is on the rise. Lamoreaux Landing's constant pursuit for superior wines has gotten the industry's attention—and the consumers'. From the crew in the vineyard to the winemaking team in the cellar, harvest at Lamoreaux is a well-choreographed work of art. Every stage of production is managed with time-proven techniques and tailored methods of winemaking—producing results truly representing Lamoreaux's cool-climate, glacier-carved vineyard sites. Four varietals have risen to the top of everyone's list: chardonnay, riesling, gewürztraminer and cabernet franc, making up a large portion of the winery's many gold medals. Most notably, Lamoreaux Landing's chardonnay received the trophy for Best New World Chardonnay in the New World International Wine Competition, beating out more than 400 entrants.

Lamoreaux Landing's 17 acres of award-winning chardonnay is surpassed only by its riesling program. With 25 acres under vine, Lamoreaux is strategically positioned to fully exploit the diversity from six different vineyard blocks of riesling, which is quickly becoming the darling grape of the Finger Lakes. With a style for every palate and occasion, Lamoreaux Landing produces rieslings that range from a food-inviting dry wine, to a semi-dry offering that shines as an aperitif, to a super-sweet ice wine—a perfect highlight for any gathering.

Top Left: Another magnificent day on Seneca Lake reveals the winery illuminated by the morning sun.
Photograph by Kristian S. Reynolds

Middle Left: The tasting room offers visitors from all over the world the opportunity to taste award-winning, cool climate wines while enjoying 30-mile views of Seneca Lake.
Photograph courtesy of Lamoreaux Landing

Bottom Left: The gold-medal gewürztraminer wait for harvest.
Photograph courtesy of Lamoreaux Landing

Facing Page: Lamoreaux Landing's Yellow Dog Riesling Vineyard is just one of three new riesling blocks planted in the last two years.
Photograph courtesy of Lamoreaux Landing

There are no disappointed wine tasters at Lamoreaux Landing, regardless of their choice. "I only release personally tested wines. They've been enjoyed on my own dinner table with locally sourced meals—sometimes from my own vegetable garden. The terroir of our wines encompass more than just the expression of site, soil and climate. They sincerely represent the hard work of the people who nurture the grapes from the vine to the bottle," boasts Mark. "Great wine paired with good food is not only conducive to making new friends, it brings old friends and family together."

2 0 0 1
ESTATE BOTTLED

LAMOREAUX
LANDING

FINGER LAKES
SPARKLING WINE
Brut
MÉTHODE CHAMPENOISE
ALC. 12.6% BY VOL. 750 ML

WINE & FARE

Lamoreaux Landing Estate-Bottled Chardonnay
(100% chardonnay)

Pair with a collection of artisan cheeses, appetizers, seafood or white meats in creamy sauces.

Lamoreaux Landing Estate-Bottled Riesling
(100% riesling)

Pair with rich, spicy or salty food—especially complements cheeses.

Lamoreaux Landing Estate-Bottled Gewürztraminer
(100% gewürztraminer)

Pair with aged cheeses, spicy Asian, Thai or Mexican cuisine.

Lamoreaux Landing Estate-Bottled Cabernet Franc
(100% cabernet franc)

Pair with grilled or roasted pork, lamb, venison and smoked cheeses.

Tastings
Open to the public daily, year-round

McGregor Vineyard

Keuka Lake

In 1971, Bob and Marge McGregor purchased pastureland on the east side of Keuka Lake in the Finger Lakes of New York. They established one of the first vineyards in the state devoted to planting Vitis vinifera, the European grapes used to make the world's finest wines. At that time a few others were planting experimental plots of vinifera but not many were betting the farm on the success of the grapes in this cool-climate region.

McGregor Vineyard is nestled on a steeply graded hillside ranging from 900 to 1,200 feet above sea level overlooking Keuka Lake. Local climate, while severe at times, is moderated by the nearby water. True pioneers of vinifera grape growing in the Finger Lakes, the McGregors planted their first vines in the early 1970s included riesling, chardonnay, gewürztraminer, pinot noir and cabernet sauvignon.

The family founded their namesake farm winery in 1980, after years of producing award-winning amateur wines and watching other vintners' commercial success with using McGregor grapes. From the first vintage to present, the estate-grown wines are some of the region's finest. The winery remains family-owned and run by Bob and Marge's son John and his wife Stacey.

Since its inception, McGregor Winery has followed the European philosophy of winemaking. Each year's production reflects the voice of the grapes, the skill of the vineyard manager and the art of the winemaker. Grown to 40 acres, the vines are managed to maintain low-level yields of hand-picked grapes, with no more than 3 tons produced per acre. The result: small batches of handcrafted wine exhibiting superior quality.

Top Left: The McGregor clan stands together: founders Bob and Marge with their son John and his wife, Stacey.

Bottom Left: Black Russian Red grapes are ready for picking.

Facing Page: A spectacular view of Keuka Lake from McGregor Vineyard comes every year in the early fall.

Estate-grown whites include riesling, gewürztraminer, chardonnay, rkatsiteli, sereksiya rosé and muscat ottonel. Small batches of sparkling wine—blanc de blanc, blanc de noir and sparkling riesling—crafted in the méthode champenoise style are also produced. Estate-grown red wines include pinot noir, cabernet franc, cabernet sauvignon, merlot and a Bordeaux-styled blend called Rob Roy Red. These reds are barrel-aged for 12 to 20 months and mature beautifully for many years. The winery also produces an unusual dry red blend called Black Russian Red.

The Black Russian Red is McGregor's crowning achievement. It is comprised of two grape varieties: saperavi and sereksiya charni. The McGregors acquired the wood for these varieties in 1978 from USDA's Dr. John McGrew in Beltsville, Maryland. Saperavi is an ancient variety, concentrated around the Black and Caspian Sea regions, specifically in Georgia, Armenia and Ukraine. Sereksiya charni is more obscure but can be found in Eastern Europe. Saperavi is grown by a few others in the United States, but as far as the McGregors know, their winery is the sole grower and producer of Sereksiya Charni in the United States and possibly the Western Hemisphere.

In addition to producing unique wines, the McGregors offer a distinctive wine tasting experience—visitors are seated in a relaxing atmosphere and served food samples to enhance their tasting. Bob and Marge started a wine club in the mid-1980s, a time when the concept was virtually nonexistent. The loyal following has grown enormously and many have been with the

Top Left: The tasting room and stone patio invite guests to have a seat at picnic tables for wine tastings while visiting the rustic winery.

Bottom Left: In addition to having a diverse selection of wines, the gift shop is stocked with many unique and local products.

Facing Page: Bales of mulching hay used to add nutrients back to the soil naturally will be rolled out between the rows of vines after harvest.

McGregor Clan Club since its humble beginnings. Food and wine events are held at the winery and most cater exclusively to club members and guests—red and white wine barrel tastings, vertical tastings, picnics and dinners coordinated with regional restaurants. Club member or not, visitors are always warmly welcomed by the McGregors and their staff. Ultimately, their goal is to grow high quality grapes, make exquisitely distinctive wines and enjoy them with all who share a passion for fine wines.

WINE & FARE

Black Russian Red
(saperavi, sereksiya charni)

Pair with venison, game dishes and dark or bittersweet chocolate.

Gewürztraminer

Pair with spicy dishes, Thai cuisine, Munster and Roquefort cheeses, or drink alone as an aperitif.

Rkatsiteli—Sereksiya Rosé

Pair with lake trout with lemon and dill, crab legs and fennel au gratin.

Pinot Noir

Pair with grilled salmon and tuna, beef tenderloin and dark chocolate truffles.

Tastings
Open to the public daily, year-round

Montezuma Winery & Hidden Marsh Distillery

Seneca Falls

Q uite possibly one of the noblest drinks in history, mead has made its way into the hands of royalty, graced the pages of history books and garnered numerous literary mentions. With its favorable flavors of satisfying sweetness, it is now inching its way up on adventurous wine lovers' lists—and their first stop is Montezuma Winery in Seneca Falls.

Winning the adoration of medieval nobility and ancient Anglo-Saxon warriors, mead is a honey wine that holds limitless potential when put to modern standards. Loved by Aristotle and celebrated by Tolstoy, this table wine lost steam in Western cultures around the 17th century, never really gaining the status it had achieved in Eastern Europe, Nordic cultures and the Middle East. Privy to its possibilities, Bill Martin turned his attention to his father's longtime beekeeping hobby, which eventually turned into a career. The response was overwhelmingly positive.

At the time, George and Virginia Martin lived on Lake Ontario with their four children, two of whom joined the family business—Bill and Ed. George had worked for a power company and maintained a semi-commercial beekeeping operation on the side. An early retirement in 1994 put extra hours in the day and turned his hobby into a full time gig, traveling with his sons to Florida, Maine and South Carolina to pollinate orange groves and blueberry fields, sell their honey and expand the cash crop. When Bill turned the honey into mead for a local Renaissance festival, the family knew they had found a niche. With the Lake Ontario location lying in the rightly named fruit belt, they began to incorporate the communities' bounty into their bottling.

Top Left: The Martin family: George, Ginny, Ed and Bill with family pets Max and Baco.

Bottom Left: Award-winning Cranberry Bog and Sparkling Mead are pleasant surprises for first-time tasters and old friends for those who have bellied up to the Montezuma bar before.

Facing Page: Springtime at Montezuma Winery is one of the most beautiful—the wildlife is abundant.

Keeping up with local farmers' harvests has been a stronghold in defining the winery's personality, continuing the practice in 2001 at their Cayuga Lake location. An ever-present relationship with nature and the Martin family shines, evidenced by the support given to regional growers and the winery's physical location: It sits on the border of the Montezuma National Wildlife Refuge. Avid hunters and nature enthusiasts, the Martins pay respect to the preserved land in the winery's name. The land functions as a temporary home to migratory fowl, most recognizably bald eagles, osprey and thousands of Canada and snow geese. Birders and novice nature-watchers alike come to feast their eyes on some of North America's most extraordinary fauna.

The 10,000-square-foot production facility produces more than 30 fruit, honey and grape wines including black currant, pear, cranberry, peach and rhubarb. After the Martins' sparkling mead brought home a double win at the Commercial Mead Championship, their indigo-hued blueberry beverage, Blue Moon, won Best Fruit Wine in an international competition while the popular Cranberry Bog has raked in four gold medals and a double gold. Tasters typically enjoy this departure from the run of the mill, offering quite a different flavor of the Finger Lakes than most

Top Right: Sweet Mead, the first of the wines produced by winemaker Bill Martin, has proved to be an award winner.
Photograph by Greg Holler

Bottom Right: Bottles of Mead, one of the oldest alcoholic beverages dating back to biblical times.
Photograph by Greg Holler

Facing Page Top: One of the largest gift shops in the area, Montezuma Winery offers an extensive selection including wine racks, wine accessories, home décor, clothing, personalized wine labels plus much more. There is something for everyone.

Facing Page Bottom Left: Several barrels of apple brandy age during various stages of the process.

Facing Page Bottom Right: American oak barrel holds the young apple brandy, giving it a golden color and adding smoothness to the finish.

wineries. But fear not, traditionalists—Montezuma Winery carries grape wines, as well. Cabernet franc, merlot, gewürztraminer, riesling and other varietals make the wine list.

With the entire family participating in Montezuma's operation, life at the winery always remains down-to-earth. Together, the family is dedicated to the success of both the winery and the community. Their proximity to the Montezuma National Wildlife Refuge gives them the perfect opportunity to educate the public and spread awareness about the region's wetland habitat. The National Audubon Society and the refuge have opened a state-owned learning center for this purpose: The Montezuma Audubon Center. Here, an educational director works with local groups to perpetuate its cause, helped by community businesses along the way—like the Martins' winery.

Always looking to expand their offerings, they added a distillery has been added to feature premium liqueurs, plus vodka and brandy made from honey, apples or other seasonal fruits. Custom built in Germany, the Christian Carl 400-liter pot still is the first of its kind in the Finger Lakes. Each batch is a hands-on process and takes on a more artistic form, producing high quality premium spirits.

Top Left: Montezuma Winery offers a variety of fruit, grape and honey wines. Its close relationship with the refuge shows in many of its unique label designs.

Bottom Left: The first of its kind in the Finger Lakes, Hidden Marsh Distillery offers tastings and sales of distilled products produced from their impressive German-crafted column pot still.
Photograph by Greg Holler

Facing Page: Guests feel welcome at Montezuma Winery with its quaint country atmosphere.

The first of these products to be released under the sister brand, Hidden Marsh Distillery, BEE Vodka is the first ultra premium vodka distilled from honey in the Finger Lakes. Unique and hand-crafted, BEE Vodka is triple-distilled in individual batches for a flawless finish, irresistibly smooth but never sweet and crystal clear with exceptional character. It promises to bee something you've never experienced before. Sip, Relax and Just Bee.

Combine these distinctive tastes with a number of neighborhood celebrations—from a Father's Day gathering to fall festivals—and suddenly it becomes obvious why visitors flock to this outdoor-lovers' paradise.

WINE & FARE

Riesling
(100% riesling)

Pair with hot, spicy foods, shellfish, poultry, fruit salad, Monterey Jack or Gouda cheese.

Cabernet Franc
(100% cabernet franc)

Pair with beef stroganoff, steak, prime rib and pasta with red sauce.

Pintail
(100% sparkling rhubarb)

Pair with talapia or mahi-mahi; pork; green, leafy salads; cheese and crackers.

Cranberry Bog
(100% cranberry)

Pair with ham, poultry—especially turkey—or serve as a mixer in a cosmopolitan or spritzer.

Tastings
Open to the public daily, year-round

Penguin Bay
Winery and Champagne House

Hector

Penguins and wine may seem like an odd pair, but the two have come together quite successfully at Penguin Bay Winery and Champagne House in Hector. As devout animal lovers, the Petersons have recognized the endangered Humboldt penguin and used their public appeal to educate visitors—all while serving fantastic wines.

While establishing their third Finger Lakes' winery, Dick, Cindy and Dave Peterson realized that this winery should really emphasize their mindful attitude toward animals. Simultaneously, the Rosamond Gifford Zoo in Syracuse had opened a penguin exhibit, showcasing the timid birds who have struggled to exist. As warm coast dwellers, the Humboldts' survival is threatened by various factors—El Niño, the fishing industry, oil spills and researchers' disruptions. Waddling into his heart, the penguins prompted Dave to seize the awareness-raising opportunity. He offered the new winery as a sponsor to the exhibit in exchange for using the feathery faces on his bottles—all while spreading the word of the waning breed. 2005 saw the alliance form, converting the Finger Lakes Champagne House to Penguin Bay Winery and Champagne House. Details of the colony's citizens are available on the winery's website, giving personal profiles of each Humboldt penguin.

Top Left: Penguin Bay features classic varietals like gewürztraminer and pinot noir as well as unique blends such as the crisp and fruity Percussion.

Bottom Left: Several of the Penguin Bay red wines are barrel aged for up to 15 months, adding richness and complexity to the wines.

Facing Page: Visitors to the winery are treated to a spectacular view of Seneca Lake from the tasting room and from the picnic area on the patio.

Amongst the slopes of Seneca Lake, just north of Watkins Glen, the Champagne House had formerly been a champagne-only tasting room—just as the name implies. Though visitors loved the notion of sampling the bubbly beverage, they clearly missed the presence of traditional wines to try. Since there were more than a handful of impressive wines on a waiting list to make it onto the roster at the other Peterson wineries—Swedish Hill and Goose Watch—there was no shortage of wines to accompany the champagne selection. Penguin Bay Wineries and Champagne House brought together the best of both worlds—guests could now have their cake and eat it, too.

There are approximately a dozen wines plus six sparkling varieties for tasting. Varietals include chardonnay, gewürztraminer, pinot grigio, riesling, pinot noir, cabernet and valvin muscat—a hybrid grape released in 2006. Appearing as signature blends are Tuxedo White, Tuxedo Red, Maroon Four and Percussion, the double-gold medaling wine at the San Francisco International Wine Competition. The white blend is a crisp, fruitful semi-dry wine with a mango and citrus nose, enticing connoisseurs with undeniably adorable penguins armed with bass drums. The Maroon Four—a favorite of Dave's—brings a little bit of Australia to New York with this shiraz-like blend. Two prominent grapes in the combination are corot noir and noiret, both premium newcomers from the development of red grapes at Cornell University. They afford the wine a black-peppery burst with blackberry notes— quickly becoming an identifiable regional flavor.

Above: The labels feature numerous fun and colorful designs that put the penguins center stage.

Facing Page: The penguin theme reflects the owners' love of animals and their sponsorship of the Humboldt Penguins exhibit at the Syracuse Rosamond Gifford Zoo.

Although the Petersons play a very obvious role in the development of the wineries, an entire network of collaboration goes on behind the scenes. Emphasizing the importance of each staff member, Dave Peterson is keenly aware that the success of the operation needs the support of everyone—the vineyard staff led by Rick Waite, the winemaking crew led by Ian Barry, the administrative team, maintenance personnel and the sales team. This group does an amazing job at keeping up the winery and vineyards, creating experiences that guests will certainly remember.

Top Left: A cottage-style tasting room overlooks the vineyards and Seneca Lake.

Bottom Left: Spacious with rustic décor, the tasting room features two large tasting bars in two separate rooms that can accommodate large groups of people without feeling crowded.

Facing Page: Sitting just 12 miles from Watkins Glen, the winery fits in perfectly with the rolling hills of the countryside.

Once a vineyard-only site for the other Peterson wineries, the land was simply too beautiful to keep to themselves. The team reflects that idea and maintains the grounds to highlight the natural beauty of the area. Daily tasting opportunities allow visitors to take advantage of the year-round, indoor-outdoor picnic area, keeping the sights accessible through all four seasons. The expanded tasting room lets wine lovers enjoy a glass while seeing all that Seneca Lake and its surroundings have to offer.

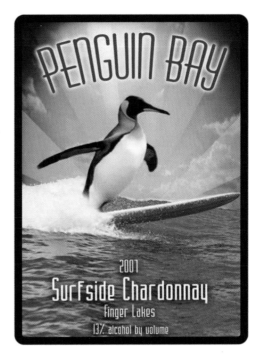

WINE & FARE

Gewürztraminer
Pair with slightly spicy Asian or Cajun fare and rich poultry—including turkey.

Maroon Four
Pair with barbecued ribs, grilled sausages and pizza.

Valvin Muscat
Pair with peach cobbler, white chocolate or fresh fruit.

Tastings
Open to the public year-round

Rooster Hill Vineyards

Penn Yan

Often overlooked as a standard farm animal in the United States, the rooster holds a great deal of virtue in Italian culture. Standing for good luck and prosperity, roosters have come to symbolize some of New York's finest vintages. With a Mediterranean influence and all the spirit of its beloved mascot, Rooster Hill Vineyards produces 100 percent regionally grown wines, resting just east of Keuka Lake. This is where the integrity and authenticity of their wines begin—in the Finger Lakes' vineyards.

Half Italian herself, owner Amy Hoffman and husband David have used Tuscany to inspire their winery, known for its ease and comfort. The couple began purchasing land in 2001, acquiring more parcels over the years to suit their grape-growing needs. When they added the tasting room and wine facilities in 2003, their future was sealed. Giving up positions in executive marketing and financial planning in Southern California, the Hoffmans jumped head-first into an industry that seems tailor-made to suit their personalities. Whether working 14-hour days through the busy weeks of autumn or planning the year's full calendar during the slow heat of summer, the Hoffmans love the demanding work. The winery sees upward of 22,000 guests each year.

Top Left: For Amy and David Hoffman, Rooster Hill Vineyards started as a hobby; now it's their passion, and the rooster symbolizes their spirit.

Bottom Left: Guests feel right at home with the beautifully crafted wines in the tasting room.

Facing Page: The big bird doesn't have to crow to let guests know that Rooster Hill is a special place.

Small, focused and intimate, Rooster Hill is a family-run operation. And never is that more clear than in the naming of the winery's prized vineyards. Gently sloping Savina Estate, a namesake parcel for Amy's great-grandmother, holds west-facing rows of riesling, cabernet franc and lemberger, specializing in pinot noir. The Catherine Estate, after Amy's great-aunt, provides the same varieties as Savina, plus gewürztraminer and vidal blanc. Between the two of them, the vineyards boast roughly 9,000 feet of drainage tile. Partially installed by the Hoffmans themselves, the tiles supply the best possible conditions for the grapes, strengthening the root structures. Future vineyards promise to take the names of David's kin, furthering their reputation in New York's wine business.

Maintaining the winemaking craft and shying away from homogeneity, Rooster Hill Vineyards embraces winemaker Barry Tortolon's ability.

With extensive studies and involvement in the wine world, Barry has been perfecting his trade since he was 15 years old. With his efforts in place, both *Wine Spectator* and *Wine Enthusiast* have taken notice of the blends and vintages. Totaling more than 200 medals, the team is most proud of the wines' international appeal. Up against some staunch competition, the Rooster Hill Riesling has beat Germany, France and Washington State for top spots.

Above Left: The Tuscan-inspired tasting room is a perfect place to enjoy premium wines.

Above Right: On the spacious patio, Rooster Hill's guests drink, taking in fine wine and a spectacular view of Keuka Lake.

Facing Page: Gracious hospitality, sweeping lake views and the very best wines in the Finger Lakes await.

Relaxing and open, the Finger Lakes region could not be more welcoming to visitors, particularly Rooster Hill. With the highest elevation overlooking the Finger Lakes, Rooster Hill has views complemented by the warm afternoon sun. As one of only two known Y-shaped lakes in the world, Keuka Lake runs 180-feet deep, making for memorable sightseeing to accompany the wine. On Saturdays, the Rooster crew fires up the outdoor pizza oven—straight from Italy—and gives visitors an added bonus: piping hot flatbread. For late-nighters, twilight tastings tempt wine lovers, offering sips of winery's finest under the stars. With an atmosphere like this and plenty of wines to taste, guests have no option but to completely unwind.

WINE & FARE

Estate Semi-dry Riesling
Pair with scallops wrapped in prosciutto.

Estate Cabernet Franc
Perfectly accompanies roast lamb.

Estate Meritage
Pair with game, roast beef, grilled duck or camembert cheese.

Tastings
Open to the public daily, seasonally

Seneca Shore Wine Cellars

Penn Yan

Hear ye, hear ye: Seneca Shore Wine Cellars is a visit to the age of chivalry and fun. Fear not, wine-loving citizens!

Eschewing wine's reputation of nose-in-the-air attitudes and arcane language, proprietor David DeMarco has shifted the focus of his winery to historical truths and fun. This emphasis is apparent upon entering, as the buildings are decorated to evoke a medieval moment. Fair maidens in costume greet the wide-eyed visitors. The inside of the tasting room is fashioned after a castle courtyard, with painted faux-stone accents and crenellations across the upper walls—a feature that once served to conceal aiming archers. Fourteen-foot cathedral ceilings show blue, puffy Michelangelo-esque clouds, and tapestries adorn the walls rendering scenes of the middle ages. Museum-replica swords, battle axes, coat-of-arms shields and knights' helmets displayed on the walls set the tone for Old World merriment.

In a world of iPods, internet and "new and improved" laundry detergent, the themed setting celebrates that which has remained the same and withstood the test-of-time. The winery and vineyards sit on the west side of Seneca Lake, where people still farm, harvest and craft wine from the land's gifts, enjoying life with friends and family. But we live in a brave new world, post 1984, post 2001. Technology has brought an array of state-of-the-art procedures and equipment to the industry. Some vintners now use ion resin exchange, off-site processing factories, protein stabilizers and even cold temperature distillation machines. Although this works for some, Mr. DeMarco believes that the best method is the one that is tried-and-true: using the techniques of the unindustrialized past when the

Top Left: David, Charlene and Caiden DeMarco take pride in their 1972 Chisholm-Ryder grape harvester. Caiden's paternal grandfather picked grapes with this machine, so now it passes to the third generation.

Bottom Left: Seneca Shore Wine Cellars has over 40 different wines available, from dry to sweet , red, rosé or white—a wine to please everyone.

Facing Page: The vineyard rises slowly from the shore. Warm lake air mixes with gentle hillside breezes to make an afternoon stroll in the vineyard a sensualist's paradise.
Photograph by John Francis McCarthy

livelihood of the farmer and the grape were one. It allows the natural flavors of the grape to shine without imposing on the age-old system of balance: balance between flavors; balance between technologies; balance between cultures; balance in health and life.

Mr. DeMarco was first struck with the idea to convert to country life while doing computer consulting work on Wall Street. During the first World Trade Center bombing in 1993, the foreboding lack of safety in Manhattan began to wear on him. With a Columbia University master's degree in computer science and 16 years in the business, Mr. DeMarco scrapped the urban life and bought the 56-acre chardonnay vineyard. A comprehensive understanding of the area's history made Mr. DeMarco excited about the returning influx of viticulture to the Finger Lakes region from its original heyday in the 1800s. Prohibition's damage had lasting effects, but the warming lakes make it a prime spot for eventual re-growth of viticulture and tourism. Since the region is centrally located to major metropolitan areas, it is simply a matter of time before the area becomes the wine basket of the Northeastern United States.

Fun, charming labels show off the spirit of the winery, picturing knights, kings, castles and nymphs. They indicate the ease and drinkability of the wine, appealing to almost every palate and offering something upbeat for any evening of the week. Most labels have stories that evoke a sense of a time-that-was; everyday life in the courtyard punctuated by feasts, royal pronouncements, or even the arrival of the dreaded royal taxman. These medieval vignettes are being organized into a collection with period artwork and history. From the crisp pinot grigio to the elusive pinot noir or the succulent merlot, there are more than 40 wines to appeal to a wide range of visitors: red to white, dry to sweet. And let's not forget riesling: the great grape of the Finger Lakes, made in three different styles.

Above Left: The original tasting room has been expanded to include museum-replica displays of medieval armor: swords, shields and helmets.

Above Right: Aging red rests in the barrel room for up to five years before careful blending and bottling. Each of the 100 barrels holds 60 gallons.

Facing Page: Rolling vineyards cascade their grapes into Seneca Shore's cellar, where they await years-long transformation into some of the state's best wine. Visitors enjoy the wine on picnics in the vineyard overlooking the beautiful lake.

Seneca Shore Wine Cellars sells 95 percent of its wine through the tasting room. Because of this, the stellar staff is the only middleman between the winemaker and the consumer, making friendliness and approachability a hallmark of the winery. Visitors do not need extensive wine knowledge to experience the enjoyment of the tasting room. Medieval-clad personnel will guide them through selections if the taster so chooses. There is no pressure. The only mandatory questions new tasters should consider answering are, "Red or white? Dry or sweet?"

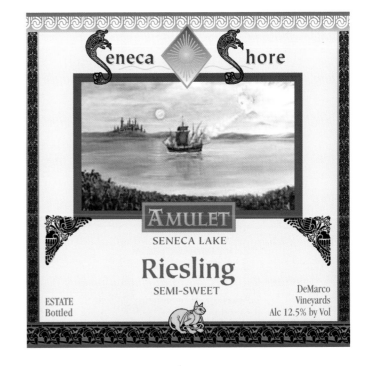

Wine & Fare

Chardonnay No-Oak

Pair with grilled wild salmon marinated in a mild mango-dill chutney.

Lemberger

Pair with seared lamb chops drizzled with demi-glace of black pepper and cherry.

Gewürztraminer

Pair with seafood risotto and a shitake-soy mushroom garnish.

Riesling Semi-Dry

Pair with a selection of soft semi-ripened cheeses and fresh fruit overlooking Seneca Lake.

Tastings

Open to the public daily, year-round

Standing Stone Vineyards

Hector

I n a picturesque region on the east side of Seneca Lake lies a pastoral farm-like setting that appears to be right out of a storybook. Standing Stone Vineyards claimed its unique name based on the legend of the Oneida Indians who were known as the "people of the standing stone." Folklore reveals the people believed that finding the standing stone meant finding perfection, including bountiful land, clear waters and sumptuous food—all in an idyllic and enduring place. Today the landowners have connected its history of place with the abundance of the future and Standing Stone Vineyards lives up to its historical roots.

Acquired by Tom and Marti Macinski in 1991, the historic rolling vineyards were run by Gold Seal Vineyards before the entrepreneurial couple transformed the more than 30-acre estate to become their viticultural dream-come-true. It once was the subject of intensive research by prior owners in the 1960s. After examining over 100 test sites for three years, early experimental plantings of riesling and chardonnay took place in 1972 and 1974. These mature grapevines now yield a healthy amount of Standing Stone's prized fruit for their acclaimed wines.

Top Left: Tom and Marti Macinski tend to their garden, just outside the tasting room door. All plants grow well here.

Bottom Left: Dessert wines Vidal Ice and Cailloux are part of the regular tasting offering at the winery.

Facing Page: The pond outside the tasting room helps provide a pastoral setting for a glass of wine.
Photograph by John Francis McCarthy

Creating and storing wine in charming renovated barn structures on the richest of land, the vineyard has proven itself as prime property for growing premium grapes and reaping harvests that produce award-winning varietals, bringing industry recognition to the Finger Lakes resort region of New York State. Its gently sloping lakeside terroir with naturally suitable, well-drained soil over slate and limestone have made it conducive to growing superior fruit, even with harsh Northeastern winters.

The winemakers produce 7,500 cases annually with upward of a dozen vintages including award-winning whites, reds and delicious dessert wines. The prolific vineyards produce a myriad of varietals from whites, including chardonnay, dry vidal, gewürztraminer and riesling, to red cabernet sauvignon, cabernet franc, pinot noir and varietals such as vidal ice and cailloux. American oak barrels impart rich red character and stainless steel tanks allow whites to stay fresh and crisp. Marti and Tom spend many hours keeping an eye over the wines' development, assuring quality of pure varietals and special blends from first crush to the final finish.

Top Left: Standing Stone Vineyards sits on the main road, making it easy to find.

Middle Left: The tasting room remains closer to the lake and away from traffic, while the old farmhouse is closer to the road.

Bottom Left: With plenty of space to relax, the tasting room invites guests to ask questions, enjoy the wine and have a drink while taking in the view.

Facing Page: Historic riesling and chardonnay vineyards provide a tranquil setting for viewing the lake and its surroundings.

Bringing notoriety to the somewhat lesser known Finger Lakes region is the mission of Marti and Tom. They strive every year to perfect their handcrafted winemaking to produce world-class wines. Currently distributing throughout New York, Washington D.C. and Virginia, the boutique vintners have plans to introduce themselves into wine and spirits stores and restaurants throughout the United States. To be sure, they have achieved critical recognition and customer satisfaction for their Standing Stone Vineyards brand and will continue to work towards perfection, like the aspirations of the area's first discoverers.

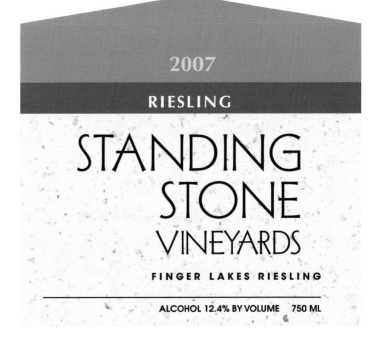

Wine & Fare

Reserve Cabernet Sauvignon

Perfect for pairing with a favorite steak, from filet mignon to steak sandwiches with garlic mayonnaise on a toasted baguette.

Pinnacle

Pair with a premium tenderloin cut, blackened rare tuna or traditional Indian cuisine with lentils.

Reserve Chardonnay

Ideally, pair with crab or lobster dishes, chicken, or fish in cream sauces.

Tastings

Open to the public daily, year-round

Swedish Hill Winery

Romulus

Where in Upstate New York would a wine lover go to have good, old-fashion fun? Undoubtedly, Swedish Hill Winery. The establishment has blended keen winemaking skills with its ability to provide out and out merriment, resulting in a fun-filled atmosphere that serves exceptional wine.

Among many of the winery's celebrations—dancing, singing and wine flow at the annual Scandinavian Festival, an opportunity used to commemorate the culture that began Swedish Hill. Dick Peterson first began making wine with his grandfather—a man who emigrated from Stockholm to western New York—when he was a young boy. Thoroughly enjoying his time spent at an uncle's farm, Dick agreed with a friend's sentiments in the 1960s to buy a small plot in the Finger Lakes and grow grapes—no vision of a winery was in mind. They sold their grapes to a large wine producer in the East for the next 15 years, honing their skills and developing a relationship with the terroir. Over time, the producer purchased fewer and fewer grapes. Building a winery to save the family vineyards seemed to be the best option. In 1985, he did just that with the help of his wife Cindy and his son Dave; the natural inclination arose to honor his heritage and give the winery a name that reflected its foundation.

Starting out with a production of merely 1,200 cases per year, Swedish Hill now holds a place as a top winemaker in the region with nearly 65,000 cases, a testimony to the staff's dedication and hard work. With the constant help of their talented teams, vineyard manager Rick Waite and winemaker Ian Barry create one of the most comprehensive wine lists, offering selections that would tempt anyone's palate. This includes mainstays

Top Left: The winery produces several dessert and brandy products including Cynthia Marie Port, Eaux de Vie Grape Brandy and Raspberry Infusion.

Bottom Left: The original vineyards date back to 1969, with older cabernet franc plantings in the area.

Facing Page: Often referred to as the "Optimus vineyard," the original planting of cabernet sauvignon, cabernet franc and merlot are used to make the winery's famed Optimus wine.

Top: With eastern shores in view, the vineyards are on the west side of Cayuga Lake, with ideal deep, high limestone soils.

Bottom: Using a state-of-the-art French mechanical grape harvest, the winery can wait until the grapes reach peak ripeness and harvest them accordingly, ensuring that the fruit is cool when processed.

Top: Among the winery buildings and vineyards, the press building sits as one of the most technologically advanced in the region.
Photograph courtesy of Swedish Hill Winery

Bottom: The barrel cellar is home to over 400 oak barrels, which are sourced from several regions within the United States, France and Hungary.

like chardonnay, riesling and cabernet franc; hybrids such as vidal blanc and Cayuga white; blends like the Bordeaux-style flagship, Optimus; plus unexpected surprises like port, sparkling wine and brandy. Fun wines have become favorites among the vineyard's repertoire like light, fruity Svenska wines in blush, white and red. The sweet riesling-like Doobie Blues—perhaps the most endearing wine—pays homage to the winery's pet miniature donkey and his talent for belting out his blues-sounding bray.

The Champagne and Dessert Wine Festival and Santa Lucia Day are two other must-see events that take place in November and December, respectively. For standard tastings, Swedish Hill is open year-round; tours run from late May to late October. Ordering is available online, by telephone and in-person during store hours. Shipping is available to most states. Buyers have the option of personalizing their wine labels with text and pictures, either from a personal pick or one provided by the winery. Lake Placid is also home to a Swedish Hill tasting room, located just on the outskirts of town in the Olympic Region. Presenting the perfect setting for wine sampling, the spacious, woodsy location offers Adirondack furniture and verdant views—all near the Olympic ski jump.

A gamut of selections coupled with an upbeat atmosphere equates to Swedish Hill being one of the most visited wineries in the Finger Lakes. The successful approach carries over to the fields, as the

Top Left: The tasting room is one of the most frequented winery stops in the region and is open daily, year-round, with winery tours given late May through October.

Middle Left: The spacious tasting room maintains a friendly, rustic charm and offers three separate tasting bars—each in a different room.

Bottom Left: Beyond the comprehensive list of wines, an extensive gift shop area lets visitors browse through a wide selection of wine-related items.

Facing Page: The vineyards grow enough grapes to make it a top producing winery in the region—all while offering second-to-none views.
Photograph courtesy of Swedish Hill Winery

wines have consistently been met with high merit. Blanc de Blanc sparkling wine is a perennial gold medal winner and a former winner of the Governor's Cup—New York's highest wine honor. Vidal Blanc received the same, as well as the title of Best New York Wine. Following suit, the Spumante Blush has brought the Best of Show distinction in the sparkling category at a handful of national and international wine competitions. Most recently, the winery itself achieved New York Winery of the Year.

Dick, Cindy and Dave later established two more wineries—Goose Watch and Penguin Bay—giving them a chance to extend their talents that began with Swedish Hill.

SWEDISH HILL

FINGER LAKES

Dry Riesling

2007
12.6% ALC. BY VOL

WINE & FARE

Dry Riesling
Pair with sea bass, chicken stir fry, turkey or smoked trout.

Blanc de Blanc
(sparkling)
Pair with sushi, Brie, spinach salad or crab cakes.

Optimus
(cabernet, merlot blend)
Pair with lamb, veal or steak.

Tastings
Open to the public daily, year-round

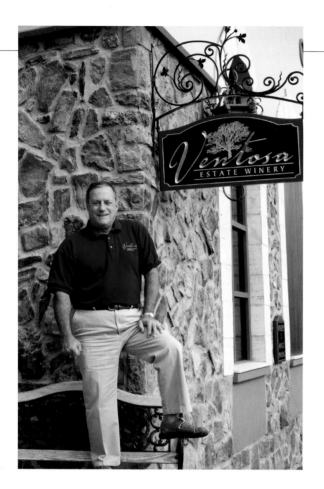

Ventosa Vineyards
Geneva

"Our mission is excellence," says Lenny Cecere, proprietor of Ventosa Vineyards—and he means it. With the modus operandi of a devout perfectionist, Lenny is putting this young winery on the map, one happy wine-drinker at a time.

Ventosa translates to windy in Italian, and the name sets the stage for the winery's Italian-inspired ambience. The Mediterranean roots of the vineyard date back to Lenny's grandfather who came to Geneva, New York, from Italy. Beer, wine and spirits were hard to come by when Prohibition and the Great Depression brought about hard times. As a tavern owner, Lenny's grandfather learned to make his own wine as a means of survival. Driven by enthusiasm, Lenny pursued his own calling with the help of his wife Mary Margaret, or Meg. After years of careful planning, they opened the 65-acre Ventosa Vineyards in 2005. Lenny moved from Fort Lauderdale, Florida, as a general contractor to pursue a goal that he, his father and grandfather shared.

Every year, Lenny and Meg return to Italy and have modeled the winery in Tuscan fashion to reflect their trips. The amber-yellow and terracotta interior of the tasting room offers an equally Mediterranean feel to the alfresco dining option on the terrace. Sitting on the northeast shore, views of Seneca Lake and the cool westerly winds keep diners company as they feast on Tuscan-inspired fare from Cafe Toscana: paninis, pizza, homemade soups, antipasti and biscotti with cappuccinos.

Rob Thomas from Shalestone Vineyards was paramount in establishing Ventosa, both in the initial set-up and current consulting with Ventosa's winemaker, Eric Shatt. This team, armed with RJ Passalacqua as the general manager, aims for 100 percent in all that they do. Excellence in the fields equates to excellence in the bottle, making any

Top Left: Lenny Cecere is the proud proprietor of Ventosa Vineyards.

Bottom Left: Guests can relax and enjoy award-winning wine on the terrace overlooking the vineyard and Seneca Lake.

Facing Page: Featured on the wine labels, a spectacular view of the vineyard and oak tree sit on Seneca Lake.

necessary sacrifice to obtain this. Giving up volume for the sake of precision, Ventosa has set a bar that it intends to keep—a sure fire way to keep each visitor pleased.

Varieties include classic options like pinot noir, cabernet sauvignon, syrah, pinot gris, riesling and chardonnay, with the riesling bringing home dozens of gold, silver and bronze medals including international, worldwide gold at a tasting competition in San Francisco in 2007. The 2007 Pinot Gris won the prestigious Cum Laude award at the 2008 Wine Literary competition held in San Francisco. For Italian vino-lovers however, there is tocai fruilano, a smooth, well-rounded northern white from Venice with notes of ruby-red grapefruit and honeydew. The sought-after Saggio—or wisdom, to Italian-speakers—is a Bordeaux blend of cabernet sauvignon, merlot and cabernet franc. Pronounced in the wine, flavors of black cherry, vanilla and tobacco complement wild game, sharp cheeses and dark chocolate. An everyday favorite is the white blend, Vino Bianco, maintaining the body of a chardonnay with the acidity of vidal and riesling. The winery goes to great lengths to perfect the wines and make certain they are enjoyed by guests.

Top Left: Charming with a touch of Old World class, the front entrance to Ventosa Vineyards gives visitors a glimpse of what is to come.

Middle Left: A front view of the Tuscan-style winery features the tasting room, Café Toscana and banquet room.

Bottom Left: The interior offers a hand-painted tasting room, as well as Café Toscana with access to the outdoor terrace.

Facing Page: The winery's lakeside terrace directly overlooks the vineyard and Seneca Lake.

Ventosa Vineyards offers one of the most unique venues for wedding receptions—La Vista e Bella room. Inside, hand-painted murals, elaborate chandeliers and wall sconces help create a European setting for the perfect day. Access to the expansive terrace allows for a stunning view of the vineyards and sunsets over Seneca Lake. Geneva's landscape and close attention to detail bring the venue to life, attracting couples from around the country—and from around the globe.

With excellence in wine, food and service, Ventosa Vineyards brings the ambience of Tuscany to the Finger Lakes.

WINE & FARE

Tocai Friulano
(100% tocai friulano)

Pairs nicely with Greek salad and white balsamic vinaigrette dressing; sunshine and a lounge chair; or sharp cheese.

Pinot Grigio
(100% estate-grown fruit)

Pair as an excellent addition to a picnic blanket, turkey sandwich and an old oak shade tree.

Cabernet Franc
(100% cabernet franc)

Pairs well with red meat and roasted potatoes or havarti cheese.

Saggio
(classic dry Bordeaux-style blend)

Pair with wild game, sharp cheeses and dark chocolate.

Tastings
Open to the public daily, year-round

Wagner Vineyards

Lodi

The Wagner family has been growing grapes in the deep glacial soils of the Finger Lakes region for five generations, resulting in an intimate connection to their land. This heritage of grape growing is the backbone of the entire Wagner Vineyards operation. Founded by owner Bill Wagner after the Farm Winery Act of 1976, Wagner Vineyards is a family-run estate-bottled winery that focuses strongly on the quality of the winemaking process from the ground up. Bill and his son John are firm believers in the fact that great wines are made in the vineyard. Rather than trying to emulate a winemaking style from another region, the winemaking process should celebrate the individual terroir of each vineyard.

Opened in 1979 and designed by Bill himself, the winery has a good deal in common with its creator: practical, ingenious and undeniably distinct. The unique octagonal building has become an icon in the region, drawing wine enthusiasts, foodies and tourists in droves—over 110,000 visitors annually. The large steep-pitched roof hangs over the winery's outer walls, shading the cellar and providing the building's recognizable façade. Within, a central tank room serves as the hub of the winemaking operation. Situated on a prime location on the eastern shore of Seneca Lake, the winery can be toured daily and while wine tasting, guests are treated to a generous view of Wagner's vinifera vineyards as well as a panoramic view of Seneca Lake and the distant horizon.

Top Left: Several 1,500-gallon American oak casks contribute to over 50,000 gallons of oak cooperage in the cellars.
Photograph by Kristian S. Reynolds

Middle Left: Wagner focuses on quality riesling along with a wide selection of other varieties—over 30 types in all.
Photograph by D. Wagner

Bottom Left: The brewing company features several standard brews: IPA, Amber Lager, Doppelbock, Oatmeal Stout, Honey Wheat and Pilsner, as well as seasonal specialties.

Facing Page: Situated on the eastern shore of Seneca Lake, the winery sits in the Finger Lakes region of Upstate New York.

It's a family operation: Bill's son John, daughter-in-law Debra, and daughter Laura are responsible for daily operations, with his six grandchildren involved as well. Winemakers John Herbert and Ann Raffetto add more than 50 years of combined experience and continuity to the Wagner team. Their wines have achieved gold and double gold medals in both national and international contests, including a recent double gold for Semi-dry Riesling at the Pacific Rim International Competition. Wagner's also has a long standing history of gold and double gold medals for their riesling, vidal and vignoles ice wines.

While Wagner Vineyards grows 225 acres of grapes comprised of 20 different varieties and produces 35 types of wine, recent efforts have been strongly committed to the future of Finger Lakes riesling. The undisputed gem of the region, riesling thrives in the well-drained glacial soils, sloping hillsides and cool nights of the Finger Lakes. Through an aggressive vineyard restructuring plan Wagner's is now the largest grower of riesling in the Finger Lakes and continues to develop innovative growing techniques to help ensure consistently high quality fruit.

Top Left: Owner and founder Stanley "Bill" Wagner, along with son John and daughter Laura.

Bottom Left: With the region's fall foliage in the background, Wagner's looks absolutely spectacular.
Photograph by Kristian S. Reynolds

Facing Page Top: The Ginny Lee offers deck dining with splendid views overlooking the vineyards and Seneca Lake.
Photograph by Kristian S. Reynolds

Facing Page Bottom Left: The winery offers something for everyone.

Facing Page Bottom Right: The Ginny Lee is a popular site for wedding receptions and other special events.
Photograph by Chesler Photography

Conversion of vinifera vineyards to the renowned Scott Henry training system has resulted in enhanced varietal characteristics due to increased light interception of the foliage and the fruit. As the winery nears its 30th anniversary, product lines are becoming more focused, honing in on the varieties of wine that people love—and the wines that the region is ideally suited to produce. While the focus of Wagner's recent activity has been the vinifera varieties, several sweeter blends including Alta B, a semi-sweet red wine named after Bill's late mother, Alta Button Wagner, continue to have strong followings.

Well known as an industry visionary in the Finger Lakes, Bill Wagner was one of the first to start a farm winery and continued his entrepreneurial ways by adding a café in 1983 and a microbrewery in 1997. The Wagner Valley Brewing Company and the Ginny Lee Café—named for Bill's only granddaughter, Virginia Lee—are established attractions on the Seneca Lake Wine Trail. The German-style brewing company offers six standard brands while the Ginny Lee serves lunch and a Sunday brunch worth writing home about: pesto garden pasta, hand-carved sirloin and a comprehensive dessert bar that would make anyone smile. The Ginny Lee is also a well-known site for wedding receptions and special events.

Top Left: A retail area displays award-winning wines and includes two Governor's Cups earned by the winery. Portraits of founder Bill Wagner and family members also hang on the walls.

Bottom Left: The winery building was designed by Bill; the unique and recognizable façade is featured in many of Wagner's wine labels.

Facing Page: Four generations have grown grapes on the prized site, overlooking Seneca Lake. The sloping hillside has recently been converted to riesling production.

A day-trip to Wagner's offers something for everyone: tours and tastings, a relaxed and friendly setting, scenic surroundings, food to savor, a wide array of wine related gifts and phenomenal wine and beer. It is a must-stop destination for anyone touring the Finger Lakes.

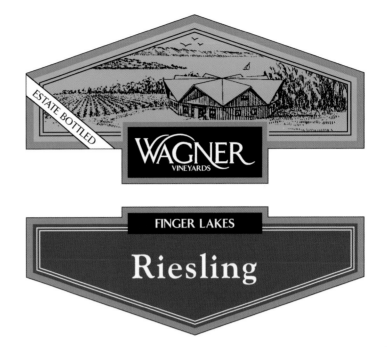

WINE & FARE

Dry Riesling
Pair with grilled fish or poultry and salads.

Cabernet Franc
Enjoy with grilled meats, pasta dishes and pizza.

Gewürztraminer
This is a perfect match for Asian or Thai foods and other spicy, flavorful dishes.

Reserve Chardonnay
Pair with flavorful seafood, poultry and pork dishes.

Tastings
Open to the public daily, year-round

White Springs Farm Estate Winery

Geneva

From good ground comes great wines. Although the first vines were planted at White Springs Winery in 2003, the farm has a long rich agricultural history dating back over 300 years. An ongoing archeological dig on the property conducted by Cornell University has uncovered the remnants of an Iroquois village whose population could have approached 2,000. The Native Americans were drawn by the abundant springs of clear white water and deep soils. Eighteenth-century residents used the springs to provide water for the growing community of Geneva located on the shores of nearby Seneca Lake. The farm surrounding the springs grew and reached a peak of 1,900 acres of fruit, cattle and other livestock in 1801. White Springs was the home of the first bottled milk plant in the region.

In the 21st century, this regional treasure is tended by a group of native New Yorkers. Carl Fribolin born in Naples, New York, purchased the farm in 1973 and used the land to raise seed corn for his seed business. Early on he felt strongly that one 50-acre side hill on the farm was ideally suited for a vineyard having been a cherry orchard in the early 1900s. So in 2003 the first vines were planted with additional vineyards developed over the next four years reaching a total of 40 acres today. The emphasis of the winery is on the aromatic white varieties that the Finger Lakes are best known for: riesling, gewürztraminer, sauvignon blanc, pinot gris and chardonnay. The red varieties pinot noir, cabernet franc, cabernet sauvignon and merlot are also grown.

Top Left: Owner Carl Fribolin and president and winemaker Derek Wilbur and have watched Carl's vision come true, helping the winery thrive for more than three years.
Photograph by Neil Sjoblom

Middle Left: White Springs produces a variety of fine reds and whites.

Bottom Left: In early June, riesling grape clusters are about to bloom.
Photograph by Neil Sjoblom

Facing Page: The hillside provides air circulation and water drainage, which are critical to growing vines young and established.

Shortly after the vines were in the ground, Carl began to assemble his team to tend the vines and make the wine. Warren Colvin joined as vineyard manager. Warren comes from Hammondsport, New York, the birthplace of the Finger Lakes wine industry. Derek Wilber joined in 2006 as president and winemaker and was joined by his brother Andrew who serves as the winery's cellar master. The two brothers grew up helping their father tend vineyards outside nearby Penn Yan. All three have been in the winegrowing business most of their adult lives. Vines are carefully pruned and trained to expose the fruit to the sun early in the season. This exposure is essential since in the cool climate of the Finger Lakes, every bit of sun and heat is vital to fully develop the desired character in the grapes, ultimately expressed in the wine.

Right: A local cabinetmaker handcrafted the tasting room's wine racks.

Facing Page Top: Visitors enjoy sipping wine on the paving stone patio; on clear days, views of Seneca Lake can be absorbed.

Facing Page Bottom Left: Visitors are welcomed with open arms to the tasting room, which boasts close proximity to the lake.
Photograph by Neil Sjoblom

Facing Page Bottom Right: A pair of brick columns marks the entrance of the tasting room, winery and farm.

The winery's tasting room and gift shop is located two miles south of the vineyard. The spacious facility overlooks Seneca Lake and features a large patio where patrons can relax and enjoy a glass of wine. Two large tasting bars crafted locally of cherry and walnut offer tasters an unhurried wine experience. In one corner a fireplace welcomes visitors in the winter. White Springs is open daily except major holidays.

Above: The circa-1900 gentleman's phaeton carriage is part of Carl Fribolin's collection.

Left: The fireplace is tucked into a corner of the tasting room.

Facing Page: Just before harvest in October, the upper riesling vineyard soaks up the sun.

The people who have joined together to write a new chapter in the long story of White Springs understand that wines reflect the place from which they grow. From vineyard to bottle, their efforts reflect a respect for the land, its history and its legacy.

White
Springs

Finger Lakes
2007

Gewürztraminer

Alc. 13.0% by Vol.

WINE & FARE

Sauvignon Blanc

Accompanies shrimp with shells in lemongrass soup—made with White Springs Sauvignon Blanc, pea shoots, cellophane noodles, olive oil and lemongrass.

Gewürztraminer

Pair with filleted lake trout, baked in olive oil, fennel, salt, ground pepper and fresh lemon juice.

Riesling

Pair with mango-pineapple salsa. Mix diced mango and crushed pineapple with chopped cilantro, shallots, lime juice, garlic clove, minced jalapeno pepper, extra virgin olive oil and salt to taste. Serve with a toasted baguette, traditional salsa chips or alongside meats and seafood.

Tastings

Open to the public daily, year-round

Freedom Run Winery, *page 280*

Niagara Landing Wine Cellars, *page 286*

Niagara

Becker Farms &
Vizcarra Vineyards
Gasport

Better than homemade, the food and wine from Becker Farms & Vizcarra Vineyards pleases all palates—from kids' to connoisseurs'. Brimming with fresh produce, this 340-acre farm has served both newcomers and devotees since 1894.

The list of produce available to guests is enough to make anyone's mouth water: strawberries, blueberries, peaches, sweet or tart cherries, raspberries, Indian corn, asparagus, onions, pumpkins, peppers, tomatoes—to name a few. And these options are only half the fun; visitors get to pick their own produce, whether off the tree or out of the ground. This has become a favorite pastime of guests, gathering families from near and far to grab a basket and enjoy the bounty of Becker Farms, lying 10 miles from Lake Ontario.

Seeing the produce put to good use is also a treat—literally. The farm serves up nine different homemade pies including, apple crumb, peach, elderberry and rhubarb. Fresh-baked cookies make the menu as well, with temptations like maple walnut, almond pillows, brownie truffles and oatmeal raisin.

After building and expanding Becker Farms for more than 20 years, Melinda and Oscar Vizcarra began to notice a pattern with their longtime patrons. Couples who had once brought their children to the farm wanted to carry on traditional visits and began expressing the idea of having an adult-only activity. Since Oscar already made wine with the farm's fruit, the couple agreed to develop a line of wines that mirrored the high-quality produce already available to visitors. With the addition, Vizcarra Vineyards was added on to the farm's name, bringing together Melinda's mother's maiden name—Becker—and Oscar's Peruvian ties.

Top Left: The Tuscan-style wine tasting bar features a rustic wine rack.

Bottom Left: Vizcarra Vineyards' award-winning wines are made from hand harvested fruit from the farm.

Facing Page: The charming sign sets a tone of welcome.
Photograph by Ester McMullen

Put off by over-sized chateaus and the high intimidation factor of wine, Melinda and Oscar wanted to bring out all of the flavorful fun without the affectation—and they succeeded. The land yields far more than just run-of-the-mill varieties; fruit from the orchards pop up on wine labels for one of the most diverse varieties in the state. Spiced Apple, Emperor Cherry, Perfect Plum, New York State Fair's gold-winning Becker Blue and Rhuberry—a cross between rhubarb and strawberry—are amongst some of the locals' favorite wines. All deliver the same sweet-tart freshness that packs incredibly fresh flavors. Wine purists can enjoy a more familiar cabernet sauvignon, riesling, Catawba or vidal blanc.

While adults sample their favorite fermented fruits, kids can choose from an impressive list of activities to busy themselves. Hayrides, pig races and apple, berry and pumpkin picking rank as some of the top favorites. Of course, kids-at-heart are certainly welcome to play, too.

Maintaining a comfortable, family atmosphere has been easy for the Vizcarras; the staff is made up of longtime employees who have become a close circle of friends. Having their daughter Amanda join the team as the events coordinator and tasting room manager has helped as well. Picnics, weddings and bridal showers can be perfectly accommodated with her help, putting the property's charm to good work.

Top Left: The fifth-generation farm is family owned and operated by Andres, Melinda and Oscar Vizcarra and Amanda Vizcarra-Crafts.

Middle Left: Unique and inviting, the tasting bar is made of antique barn beams and creates a relaxed atmosphere.

Bottom Left: Used primarily for private events and parties, the second tasting room features a beautiful stained glass monogram.

Facing Page: The entry courtyard doubles as a reception area for weddings and special events.

The tasting room is connected to an old apple barn, structured with massive barn beams and accented with reclaimed tile, adding a perfectly elegant touch.

Whether accompanied by a glass of wine or a slice of pie, kids, couples, families and singles will find the perfect mixture of relaxation and good taste at Becker Farms & Vizcarra Vineyards.

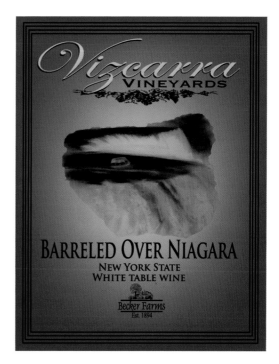

WINE & FARE

Emperor Cherry
(100 % cherry)

Drink as an after-dinner wine or pair with dark chocolate, cheesecakes or savory lamb dishes.

Red Creek Raspberry
(100% raspberry)

Pair with fresh fruit, summer tarts and light custards, or enjoy it as a dessert wine.

Quaker Red Rougon

Pair with pasta and robust cheeses like pepper jack or aged gorgonzola—perfect for sipping.

Erie Canal Catawba

Pair with appetizers and light meals, especially on warm summer days.

Tastings
Open to the public daily, year-round

Freedom Run Winery

Lockport

As children growing up in Lockport, brothers Larry, Chip and Sean Manning spent idyllic summers amongst the peach trees and apple orchards on the farms surrounding their childhood home. A favorite spot was a farm nestled against the bench of the Niagara Escarpment—a limestone formation that marks the shoreline of a prehistoric lake—and they often gave chase among the trees, playing the games of boyhood that would create memories to last a lifetime. But they had no idea of the future that lay beneath their feet. So it was almost fate when the property went up for sale decades later and the trio began discussing the prospect of a purchase. Soon afterward, the idea for Freedom Run Winery was born.

This is a family operation in every sense of the words, with each of the Mannings bringing their respective expertise to Freedom Run. From the beautiful tasting room adorned with Sean's hand-thrown pottery to Chip's agricultural acumen on display in the vineyard—not to mention Larry's, along with his wife Sandra's, stamp on the handcrafted wines—the family's warm spirit and generous personality can be felt everywhere.

With the winery named for the nearby Underground Railroad path that led fleeing slaves into Canada—they often ran along the escarpment at night, shielded among the trees from their would-be captors—the word 'freedom' holds more than its literal meaning for the Mannings. To them, the liberty of sharing their passions with the world, along with expressing a love of family, wine, art and community, is the very epitome of the word.

Top Left: Co-owner Larry Manning with his wife Sandra maintain the winery.

Bottom Left: Bottles and French oak barrels line the winery's production facility.
Photograph by Leary Studios

Facing Page: The apple orchard and upper vineyards have clay-heavy soils and steep slopes, yielding distinctly concentrated grapes.

The land itself has become a member of the family in its own right, commanding respect and admiration for its beauty and productivity. Sitting against the bench of the escarpment with 200-foot elevations in both directions, Freedom Run is surrounded by nature's art: acres of vibrant apple orchards, green vineyards and slightly sloping hills that were once filled with golden wheat. Named by Cornell University as the next hot spot for grape growing, the Niagara Escarpment offers fertile soil that consists of neutral clay over limestone, not to mention fruit-friendly growing conditions—with peach trees in abundance. Indeed, agriculturalists know that if peaches can thrive, grapes will follow suit. The escarpment also features well-drained soils, sufficient slope, a steady but moderate water supply and an extended ripening season, thanks to the symbiotic relationship between the escarpment and the deep waters of Lake Ontario.

As a result of the growing conditions, Freedom Run has been able to produce a roster of exceptional estate wines—which include merlot, cabernet sauvignon, cabernet franc, chardonnay, riesling and pinot noir. The up-and-coming star of Freedom Run, however, is its version

of champagne: Seanpagne. Soon to be a well-known signature, the family has given a wink and a nod to Sean for his hard work in making Freedom Run a reality and has named the release in his honor. A stone house on the property—built in 1826—will showcase the sparkling wine as Freedom Run's adjunct tasting room.

Above: The tasting room boasts the artwork and craftsmanship of each of the Manning brothers.
Photograph by Leary Studios

Right: Chip Manning co-owns the winery and serves as vineyard manager.
Photograph by Leary Studios

Facing Page Top: Freedom Run's historic barn dates back to 1826 and now hosts weddings, parties and community gatherings.
Photograph by Leary Studios

Facing Page Bottom: The barn's interior has been restored to its former glory, using original designs and materials.

Perpetually giving back to the area that has done so much for them, the Mannings offer an array of art to interested visitors—a passion that has been perpetuated by avid art enthusiast Sandra and artist Sean. These days, Sean, who divides his time between Lockport and St. Petersburg, Florida, spends a good portion of his free time at the potter's wheel in his on-site artist's studio, shaping clay into pieces that adorn the winery's exceptional tasting room. Though he scoffs with no small measure of discomfort when people use the word "visionary" to describe him, there is no denying the vision it took to bring Freedom Run Winery to life. And he isn't done putting his stamp on Freedom Run by a long shot.

Here, wine is also an art form, and it is put on display for visitors to observe during production. A large glass wall allows spectators the chance to peek into the process, gaining access to the winery's daily operations. To really get a feel for a vintner's life, guests are encouraged to try a barrel tasting and to become a member of the Private Barrel Club. As a member, they have the opportunity to harvest, crush and press their grapes, then ferment, filter, bottle and label all of their hard work. It is a priceless experience for wine lovers, and one of the many reasons that Freedom Run remains one of New York's favorite wineries.

Above Left: Co-owner Sean Manning enjoys spending a great deal of time at the potter's wheel.
Photograph by Leary Studios

Above Right: Sean's work is on display throughout the winery and exclusively available for sale in the tasting room.
Photograph courtesy of Freedom Run Winery

Facing Page: Dating back to the 1820s, the original stone house is the soon-to-be home of Seanpagne, where the Mannings will pour estate sparkling wines and host group events and parties.
Photograph by Leary Studios

At Freedom Run, all of the Mannings know that good wines start with good fruit, offering wines made with vinifera as well as hybrid and native grapes from the heart of the Niagara Escarpment. A hands-on business in every sense of the word, the family lives by a few tenets: good wines, good friends and good conversation. It is what has shaped the winery so far—and what will inform its future.

Freedom Run
WINERY & VINEYARDS

WINE & FARE

Riesling
Pair with crab bisque.

Meritage
Accompanies peppercorn-crusted beef tenderloin.

Semi-Dry Riesling
Pair with chicken apple curry.

Pinot Noir
Pair with grilled wild salmon.

Tastings
Open to the public daily, year-round

Niagara Landing Wine Cellars

Cambria

N iagara: the word brings to mind strength, wonder—and for many—home. Because of this, no better name would suit the county's first winery: Niagara Landing Wine Cellars.

Sitting amongst vineyards that date back to the 1800s, the winery lies on the glacially deposited land that supplies its thriving grapes. Just east of the roaring Niagara Falls and south of Lake Ontario, Niagara Landing could not offer a better location to travelers and sightseers. The locals have no complaints, either.

Now in its third generation of the Smiths' management, co-owners and siblings Peter Smith and Jacqueline Smith Connelly care for the property with the help of their family. Pete manages the vineyards and works with winemaker Domenic Carisetti. After years of work with big East Coast wine companies, Domenic wanted something more personal, grass roots. And the Smiths' wine cellars proved an ideal spot. Domenic's complete control of the grapes is what gives the varietals rich, memorable flavors.

Grapes from the Niagara Landing vineyards run the full gamut, native Vitis labrusca and hybrid. Concord, Niagara and steubens are found alongside vidal blanc and Cornell experimentals like newly trademarked Rubiana. Naturally, the winery also produces cabernet sauvignon, riesling, chardonnay and merlot. The flat land works well for the native grapes, and the bench of the escarpment for more tender varietals, growing just 10 miles west of the Niagara River near the nutrient-full escarpment.

And what goes better with wine than straight-from-the-garden herbs? Lavender, sage, thyme, basil, rosemary and cilantro are a few of the characters that sprout up for a

Top Left: An early-summer herb garden with lavender, chives and sage has a healthy start, while native Catawba vines trellis in the center.

Bottom Left: Elegant and peaceful, the edge of the vineyard is an ideal setting for a wine and cheese tasting.

Facing Page: Peek beneath the arched canopy of walnut trees and across the road to vineyards bursting with leaves and blossoms.

visit on the property's garden, not to mention the heirloom tomato plantings. Guests are welcome to snip and sniff their favorites, guided by hand-painted round stones from Lake Ontario serving as labels for each plant. Inside, the staff welcomes questions about recipes and offers wine pairing and cooking advice—including wine appreciation workshops, an introduction to winemaking seminar and Evenings with the Winemaker: a chance to sample about-to-be-released wines paired with foods prepared by local chefs. The gallery shows off watercolors, acrylics and drawings by regional artists.

Producing the Niagara Escarpment's first estate-grown ice wine, the Smiths have received a good deal of recognition for their cold-climate delight. The grapes retain a distinct balance between acidity and sweetness due to the harvesting technique. Grapes are left on the vine to freeze and are harvested thoroughly frozen. Pressing removes excess moisture in the form of ice, leaving concentrated fruit and sugar solids to flavor the wine. "An enchanting mingling of tropical fruits, mango, papaya and apricot with a lingering hint of honey," reads the Niagara Landing Vidal Blanc Ice Wine label. Port and Chocolate Dream are also house specialties.

The Smiths make hospitality look easy; and maybe because they have such a longstanding, personal investment in the area. Jackie and Pete's father owns a private airfield just across from the vineyards.

Top Left: Three generations stand with the winemaker. From left to right, the family includes: Sarah and Bob Wasik, 4th generation; winemaker Domenic Carisetti; Ray Smith seated, 2nd generation; Pete Smith, 3rd generation; friend Myrna Miller; Mike and Jackie Smith-Connelly, 3rd generation; Kay and Rob Fetter, 4th generation.

Bottom Left: The path leads visitors by flowerbeds full of Grandma's favorites and a shady respite on the way to the front door, guaranteeing a warm welcome into the tasting room.

Facing Page: Vintage aircrafts are on display each weekend during the summer months. A 1937 Stearman is owned and was restored by Ray Smith, painted with the official Army specifications and featured on a wine label.

Smithfield is home to the Niagara Soaring Club. On a warm summer day, guests can lift their eyes to the sky, watching and listening for a *whoosh* as a glider passes overhead. There is also a group of gentlemen devoted to spending many hours restoring pre-World War II aircrafts—the most historic being a 1935 Porterfield and 1937 Stearman, which is featured on the label of the wine bearing its name: Stearman Steuben.

As the oldest winery and founder of the Niagara Wine Trail, Niagara Landing Wine Cellars has made community and reputation hallmarks of its establishment, ensuring staying power for the next generations.

WINE & FARE

Vidal Blanc Ice Wine
*Pair with salted, roasted nuts and aged
New York State Cheddar cheese.*

Baco Noir
*Pair this dry red with venison, lamb or steak entrées
or pasta in a light tomato sauce.*

Misty Niagara
*Serve ice cold over sliced fresh peaches or with
pizza and authentic Buffalo chicken wings.*

Chocolate Dream Mexican Sundae
*This dessert wine can be served over vanilla ice cream
with roasted peanuts and whipped cream.*

Tastings
Open to the public daily, year-round

The Winery at Marjim Manor

Appleton

What's the difference between wine and spirits? Wine is what you taste at The Winery at Marjim Manor; spirits are who you meet. The historical background of the building is just part of the fascination of this unique location.

After graduating from Cornell University, Margo and Jim Bittner settled in western New York, became dairy farmers and raised three children. The prefix for their registered Holstein herd was the blending of their two names, Marjim.

In 1989, the Bittners' operation shifted to fruit farming. Eventually, Jim formed a partnership with Tom Singer, continuing his family's operation, Singer Farms. The farm became well known for its apples, sweet cherries, tart cherries, apricots, plums, prunes, peaches and nectarines. One of the markets Jim developed was fruit wineries. Before long, Jim and Margo were wondering how to open a winery themselves.

In 2003, the building housing the manor came up for sale, Margo created a marketing plan and the winery seeds were planted. At the time she opened the winery, she was one of two WOW—woman operated wineries—in New York State. In addition to making a range of fruit wines, she learned the mysterious background of the building. Soon the wines had names like Lord of the Manor, Thursday Afternoon at Three, Fifty Windows and 100 Windows. There is even the Cat's Meow in honor of the manor felines and True Blue for the dog lovers.

Top Left: One of very few in the state, this WOW—woman operated winery—is owned by Margo Sue Bittner.

Bottom Left: A Pear Made In Heaven is an award-winning wine that flows into buttery richness with a hint of spice and smooth pear finish.
Photograph by Krista Beth Feltz

Facing Page: The elegance and charm of the manor makes any event memorable.
Photograph by Krista Beth Feltz

Visitors to the manor hear the story as they enjoy the wines. From builder Shubal Merritt, to Dr. Charles Ring, to the Sisters of St. Joseph, the story glides through the past 150 years. Guests never know when a family member, spirit or live, will come through and share a story as well.

The staff shares various wine and food pairing tips. For example, the dry Plum Dandy is wonderful with spicy food; Cranberry Crescendo pairs with turkey. There are wine and food pairing classes and dinners held on a regular basis.

With a chapel inside and beautiful grounds, many weddings and reunions are held at the manor. Margo can perform the ceremony, making the facility full service.

Margo is fond of saying that she is the typical American Farmer—college educated, involved in a family operation, and concentrating on one product. In addition to buying the fruit from her husband, daughter Janet works at the winery full time. Older son Kevin works with the winemaker when he is not busy at Singer Farms. Both Kevin and Janet followed their parents to Cornell. Purdue Boilermaker David, the youngest, is considering coming home to the farm as well.

Top Left: The winery is a historical Niagara County landmark, which gained a reputation 100 years ago as a haunted house.
Photograph by Krista Beth Feltz

Bottom Left: Scenic grounds are perfect for photos, outdoor ceremonies and receptions.
Photograph by Krista Beth Feltz

Facing Page: The Winery at Marjim Manor specializes in wines that are flowing and soft on the palate, like Plum Dandy, Cranberry Crescendo and Treasure Beyond Measure.
Photograph by Krista Beth Feltz

What is the difference between wine and spirits? Visit The Winery at Marjim Manor to learn all the details.

The Winery at Marjim Manor, where history and charm always surround you.

WINE & FARE

Cherry Concerto
Pair with a variety of chocolates or turkey—perfect around the holidays.

Heart of Gold
(apricot)
Pair with lamb, spicy stuffing, sage dressing, and sweet and sour ham.

Treasure Beyond Measure
(plum)
The sweet wine pairs well with spicy Asian dishes or spiced breads, especially gingerbread.

Tastings
Open to the public daily, year-round

Merritt Estate Winery, *page 300*

Vetter Vineyards Winery, *page 304*

Erie

Mazza Chautauqua Cellars

Mayville

Why would anyone leave the Italian countryside, dotted with fig orchards and chestnut groves? Visit Mazza Chautauqua Cellars in New York's wine region and the answer becomes clear. With a backdrop to rival Italy's, the cellars offer more than a typical winery experience, bringing together a distillery, a café and an appreciation for fine wines beneath one roof.

With food and drink as charming as its owners, Mazza Chautauqua Cellars is the result of a Mazza family journey. As children, brothers Frank and Robert Mazza left the fruit-rich countryside of Calabria, Italy, to later establish a winery in northwestern Pennsylvania. Though trained as engineers, the duo gained hands-on experience from years of working in vineyards, affording them a realistic vision of the labor that goes into every bottle. Successful and satisfied with the growth of his business, Robert, along with his wife Kathleen and adult children, Mario and Vanessa, expanded the operations to New York 32 years later in 2005. Built to display its Mediterranean roots, Mazza cellars exudes a European air; the warm-hued stucco exterior and gentle arches stand out on Chautauqua's picturesque lakeside. Meanwhile, the building strives for ecological friendliness, showcasing features such as geothermal heating and cooling, recycled building materials and energy-efficient lighting.

Top Left: Award-winning wines can be enjoyed with fresh lunch fare in the open-air café.

Bottom Left: The handmade Christian Carl pot still rises through the floor to greet visitors.

Facing Page: The entrance along Route 33 near Mayville directs patrons to the winery, distillery and café.

Sourcing grapes from growers in the Lake Erie region and across New York, Mazza produces a range of table, premium and specialty wines under winemaker Gary Mosier. Most heavily awarded, the Ice Wine of Vidal Blanc has brought the Mazza family more than a dozen medals in recent contests like the Los Angeles International and Finger Lakes competition. And it is no wonder judges have taken notice; the winery has devoted more than 24 years to perfecting the craft of ice wine.

Home to the only distillery in western New York, Mazza Chautauqua Cellars makes brandy and spirits from only the highest quality grapes and fruit including cherries, plums, pears and apples. Sparked by dinnertime conversation around the family table, the idea for a distillery was put into motion by Mario Mazza, on-site enologist who completed his post graduate education in the art of winemaking and grape-growing in South Australia. The star of the distillery however, is the German-import hand-crafted copper pot still. From here, the boutique operation makes grappa and eau de vie in addition to brandy. Treated with as much care as the wine, the distiller focuses on aroma and flavor throughout the process to ensure that the product lives up to the Mazza name.

Top Left: Mazza Chautauqua Cellars produces not only wine, but also specialties like eau-de-vie—fruit brandy—ice wine and port.

Middle Left: Making wine is a family affair for the Mazzas: Vanessa, Kathleen, Robert, Mario and Melissa, Mario's wife.

Bottom Left: Wine and distilled beverages can be sampled in the warm and spacious tasting room.

Facing Page: The building's Mediterranean architecture is reminiscent of the family's Italian heritage, yet showcases numerous modern and green features.

Hungry? A fresh-pressed panini from the café is worth the trip alone—perfect with a glass of wine, of course, and even more enjoyable when savored at a table in the open-air café overlooking a picturesque pond. And if visitors are looking for a variety of activities after their drinks, the Chautauqua Institution sits directly across the street. Boosting local tourism and providing a place of reflection, the institution is a national historic landmark and center for cultural activities. Mazza Cellars is a place where people come to relax and enjoy regional offerings—so grab a glass of wine and kick up your feet.

MAZZA CHAUTAUQUA CELLARS

Riesling
LAKE ERIE 20/05
750ML 12% ALC.BY VOL.

WINE & FARE

Riesling
(100% riesling)
Pair with leek and tofu oyster-mushroom sauté.

Pinot Grigio
(100% pinot gris)
Pair with oven-poached salmon fillets.

Forte of Cabernet Franc
(ruby style port)
Best served with Stilton cheese or dark chocolates.

Tastings
Open to the public daily, seasonally

Merritt Estate Winery

Forestville

What really makes visitors feel welcome? As guests walk through the front door of Merritt Estate Winery, a few things elicit immediate warmth: a smiling face, a glass of wine and the undoubted affection of the family dog. Visitors instantly feel like old family friends, revealing the winery's laid back atmosphere and charm.

Now run by Jason Merritt and his father William, Merritt Estate is the result of generations working in the grape and wine trade. The vineyards have been in the family since the 19th century, prompting William to strongly pursue the industry with the help of both his father and brother. The Farm and Winery Act of 1976 dramatically raised the financial feasibility of operating a winery, removing many licensing fees and allowing farms to sell products directly to consumers. This gave the family the boost they needed, turning the property into a full-fledged winery that same year. Once one of only a handful, Merritt Estate now sits among 21 wineries in the region, as well as over 250 in the state.

The winery shows off a steel exterior, a building that has grown and expanded with the business over the years. Beneath, the gravelly, clay-based soil yields ideal fruit. Sitting on the 45th parallel, the vineyards share latitude with the Bordeaux and Champagne regions of France, affording similar growing climates. Melted glaciers have left behind nourishment for area vines, allowing roots to grow deep into the earth. Labrusca, concord and French hybrids have done very well under the Merritts' supervision; the estate sells nearly 65,000 gallons of wine annually. Merritt Estate's Bella Rosa serves as the perfect example of a sweet red, bringing all the flavor of the land into the bottle.

Top Left: Owners William T. Merritt, Jason C. Merritt, son Joshua C. Merritt and their Rottweiler Butch, love the winery as if it were a member of the family.
Photograph by Jason C. Merritt

Bottom Left: A Sweet lambrusco-style red, Bella Rosa, holds the title of the most decorated wine.

Facing Page: The marquis in front of Merritt Winery announces visiting hours.

Active in all things community, the Merritts have orchestrated countless events to promote charity and local awareness through their business. Local celebrities and sports figures like Buffalo Sabres goaltender Ryan Miller and his Steadfast Foundation; Buffalo Bills Hall of Fame quarterback Jim Kelly and the Hunter's Hope Foundation; Buffalo Bills punter Brian Moorman and the P.U.N.T. Foundation; and most recently, former Buffalo Bills tight end Kevin Everett and his Kevin Everett Foundation have helped the winery raise money for their individual charities. Juvenile Diabetes Research Foundation, the American Heart Association and Roswell Park Cancer Institute have also made the list. Fairs, festivals and events provide nonstop fun for the winery: Septemberfest and Strawberry Festival are seasonal events held at the winery. The Taste of Buffalo, Taste of Rochester and Taste of Syracuse and the New York State Fair are examples of the events that Merritt estate is involved with as well. America's Grape Country Wine Festival began when Bill and Jason realized that it was nearly impossible to sample a variety of the region's wines without a hefty travel investment. Merritt Estate brings several wineries, craft and food vendors under one roof for people to taste, promoting local agriculture and cuisine.

Top Left: A photograph of Merritt homestead, circa 1895, reveals the winery's history.
Photography courtesy of Merritt Estate Winery

Middle Left: The picnic pavilion holds caterings and functions of all sizes, including weddings up to 400 people.

Bottom Left: Merritt's present day homestead holds just as much charm as it did more than a century ago.

Facing Page: Leading to the winery's original barn, the driveway lets visitors take in the fertile surroundings of New York's countryside.

And if all this is not enough to satisfy wine lovers and gourmets, the winery caters special events and gatherings for any occasion. Formally trained in culinary arts himself, Jason knows that good food is intrinsically linked with wine. Providing both of these offers guests the opportunity to have an all-out experience when visiting the estate, whether for a family reunion, wedding reception or an impromptu tasting.

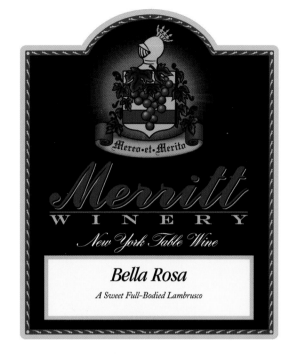

Wine & Fare

Winemaster's Choice
(cabernet sauvignon, cabernet franc and merlot)

Pair with an array of hearty dishes like shrimp and crab cannelloni in a cream sauce, pecan-crusted swordfish in a rosemary-butter sauce or medium-spiced curry entrées.

Bella Rosa
(sweet lambrusco-style red wine)

Perfect for any occasion. Enjoy chilled, alone or with friends. Bella Rosa is also excellent with highly flavored pasta dishes.

Chardonnay

Pair with lamb shanks, braised with onions, thyme, garlic, white wine vinegar, served alongside white bean puree. Fish like halibut, trout and mahi-mahi work, as well.

Tastings
Open to the public daily, year-round

Vetter Vineyards Winery

Westfield

The family at Vetter Vineyards Winery is the same as anyone else's. Except they run a farm, production facility, retail shop and shipping center in order to make and distribute premium, high quality New York wines. With five children and a successful winery, Mark and Barbara Lancaster never see a dull moment. Born and raised in Chautauqua County, the couple maintains 100 acres of Lake Erie farmland in their hometown. All the dedication and hard work pays off in the bottle, reflecting just how much flavor can come from a boutique winery.

Vetter Vineyards first began when Craig Vetter opened the business in 1987. As time went on, he thought selling the operation would be in the best interest of everyone involved. And the Lancasters were the perfect family to take over. Mark grew up with the vintner lifestyle, making wine and tending to the vineyards since an early age. While working as a general manager and winemaker at another New York facility, Mark decided to lay down his own roots and start working for himself, purchasing the Vetter property in 2003. With Barbara's experience of working in the industry since 2001, the two now make an ideal business pair. Mark and Barbara use every minute wisely, managing everything from administrative duties and marketing to farm labor and shipping—not to mention rearing the five children.

Top Left: Not only is there a beautiful winery and vineyard at Vetter Vineyards, there are five wonderful children.

Bottom Left: The premium wines come in many shapes and sizes.

Facing Page: In May, vines begin coming to life at the scenic hillside location.

With a 25-acre parcel dedicated to growing more than 20 types of grapes, the vineyards sit at the foot of the Allegheny Plateau amongst the land's rolling hills. Varying soils and moderated temperatures from Lake Erie create an atmosphere that allows a range of grapes to grow. Vetter Vineyards' stock includes shiraz, riesling, merlot, cabernet sauvignon, pinot noir, pinot grigio and cabernet franc. Perhaps the most interesting of the bunch however, is the zweigelt. This Austrian grape does not appear in any other vineyard portfolio in the area. Resulting wines offer a medium-body with mild spiciness and notes of red and dark berries—a drink visitors will remember. Premium red wines remain the cornerstone of Vetter Vineyards, producing the highest quality bottles of reds. As the years continue, the Lancasters plan on expanding the wine list to include even more noteworthy selections.

Top Left: As visitors come into the parking area, they cannot help but admire the old red barn, where the sun is always shining.

Bottom Left: As guests walk down the vineyard lane, Dutchess is just one of 20 grape varieties they meet.

Facing Page: Everyone can enjoy a glass of wine and listen to the birds, while taking in the amazing countryside.

The best way to experience Vetter Vineyards Winery is to visit; guests always feel like family. Avid outdoors people, the family may be spotted hiking, hunting, playing or fishing bass from their pond. The beautiful wooded area offers something for nearly everyone, including picnic tables perched above the vineyards; a perfect spot for sipping handmade, hand-bottle wines. Events take place year-round, including music festivals at the winery and off-site visits to local restaurants, where the Lancasters team up with chefs to give diners an opportunity to sample their finest.

PINOT NOIR
Dry, light oak with mixed black fruit.
NEW YORK STATE
VETTER VINEYARDS WINERY
Grown, produced and bottled by Vetter Vineyards Winery: 8005 Prospect Station Rd. • Westfield, NY 14787 • BW 731

WINE & FARE

Pinot Noir
Pair with young spring vegetables and fresh herbs.

Zweigelt
Pair with seared fish, poultry and vegetables.

Chardonnay
Pair with roasted chicken with cream sauce and walnuts.

Riesling
Diverse and table friendly, pair with creamy soups, fish and poultry. Or try it with fruity side dishes such as slices of baked apples.

Tastings
Open to the public year-round

Spectacular Wineries of New York

New York Team

Regional Publisher: Kathryn Newell

Graphic Designer: Kendall Muellner

Editor: Katrina Autem

Production Coordinator: Laura Greenwoood

Headquarters Team

Publisher: Brian G. Carabet

Publisher: John A. Shand

Executive Publisher: Phil Reavis

Director of Development & Design: Beth Benton Buckley

Director of Book Marketing & Distribution: Julia Hoover

Publication Manager: Lauren B. Castelli

Senior Graphic Designer: Emily Kattan

Graphic Designer: Ashley Rodges

Editorial Development Specialist: Elizabeth Gionta

Managing Editor: Rosalie Z. Wilson

Editor: Anita M. Kasmar

Editor: Daniel Reid

Managing Production Coordinator: Kristy Randall

Production Coordinator: Drea Williams

Traffic Coordinator: Meghan Anderson

Administrative Manager: Carol Kendall

Administrative Assistant: Beverly Smith

Client Support Coordinator: Amanda Mathers

PANACHE PARTNERS, LLC

CORPORATE HEADQUARTERS

1424 Gables Court

Plano, TX 75075

469.246.6060

www.panache.com

Brotherhood, America's Oldest Winery, *page 110*
Photograph by Tomas Donoso

Hunt Country Vineyards, *page 200*

Index of Wineries

Americana Vineyards & Winery
4367 East Covert Road
Interlaken, NY 14847
607.387.6801
www.americanavineyards.com

Atwater Estate Vineyards
5055 State Route 414
PO Box 216
Hector, NY 14841
607.546.8463
www.atwatervineyards.com

Becker Farms & Vizcarra Vineyards
3724 Quaker Road
Gasport, NY 14067
716.772.2211
www.beckerfarms.com

Bedell Cellars
36225 Main Road
Cutchogue, NY 11935
631.734.7537
www.bedellcellars.com

Belhurst Winery
4069 Route 14 South
PO Box 609
Geneva, NY 14456
315.781.0201
www.belhurst.com

Benmarl Winery
156 Highland Avenue
Marlboro, NY 12542
845.236.4265
www.benmarl.com

Brotherhood,
America's Oldest Winery, Ltd.
PO Box 190
100 Brotherhood Plaza Drive
Washingtonville, NY 10992
845.496.3661
www.brotherhoodwinery.net

Bully Hill Vineyards
8843 Greyton H. Taylor Memorial Drive
Hammondsport, NY 14840
607.868.3610
www.bullyhill.com

Casa Larga Vineyards
2287 Turk Hill Road
Fairport, NY 14450
585.223.4210
www.casalarga.com

Castello di Borghese
Vineyard and Winery
17150 Route 48 at Alvah's Lane
PO Box 957
Cutchogue, NY 11935
631.734.5111
800.734.5158
www.BorgheseVineyard.com

Comtesse Thérèse
Union Avenue
PO Box 2799
Aquebogue, NY 11931
631.871.9194
www.comtessetherese.com

Constellation Brands
207 High Point Drive, Building 100
Victor, NY 14564
585.678.7100
www.cbrands.com

Dr. Konstantin Frank's Vinifera
Wine Cellars
9749 Middle Road
Hammondsport, NY 14840
607.868.4884
www.drfrankwines.com

Duck Walk Vineyards
PO Box 962
231 Montauk Highway
Water Mill, NY 11976
631.726.7555
www.duckwalk.com

Fox Run Vineyards
670 State Route 14
Penn Yan, NY 14527
315.536.4616
800.636.9786
www.foxrunvineyards.com

Freedom Run Winery
5138 Lower Mountain Road
Lockport, NY 14094
716.433.4136
www.freedomrunwinery.com

Glenora Wine Cellars
5435 Route 14
Dundee, NY 14837
607.243.5511
www.glenora.com

Goose Watch Winery
5480 Route 89
Romulus, NY 14541
315.549.2599
www.goosewatch.com

Hermann J. Wiemer Vineyard
3962 Route 14
PO Box 38
Dundee, NY 14837
607.243.7971
www.wiemer.com

Heron Hill Vineyards
9301 County Route 76
Hammondsport, NY 14840
607.868.4241
www.heronhill.com

Hunt Country Vineyards
4021 Italy Hill Road
Branchport, NY 14418
800.946.3289
www.huntwines.com

Jason's Vineyard
1785 Main Road
Jamesport, NY 11958
631.926.8486
www.jasonsvineyard.com

Keuka Spring Vineyards
243 Route 54
East Lake Road
Penn Yan, NY 14527
315.536.3147
www.keukaspringwinery.com

King Ferry Winery
658 Lake Road
King Ferry, NY 13081
315.364.5100
www.treleavenwines.com

Knapp Winery
2770 Ernsberger Road
Romulus, NY 14541
607.869.9271
www.knappwine.com

Lamoreaux Landing Wine Cellars
9224 Route 414
Lodi, NY 14860
607.582.6011
www.lamoreauxwine.com

Martha Clara Vineyards
6025 Sound Avenue
Riverhead, NY 11901
631.298.0075
www.marthaclaravineyards.com

Mazza Chautauqua Cellars
4717 Chautauqua-Stedman Road
Mayville, NY 14757
716.269.3000
mcc.mazzawines.com

McGregor Vineyard
5503 Dutch Street
Dundee, NY 14837
607.292.3999
www.mcgregorwinery.com

Merritt Estate Winery
2264 King Road
Forestville, NY 14062
716.965.4800
www.merrittestatewinery.com

Millbrook Vineyards & Winery
26 Wing Road
Millbrook, NY 12545
845.677.8383
800.662.WINE
www.millbrookwine.com

Montezuma Winery
& Hidden Marsh Distillery
2981 Auburn Road
Seneca Falls, NY 13148
315.568.8190
www.montezumawinery.com
www.beevodka.com

Niagara Landing Wine Cellars
4434 Van Dusen Road
Lockport, NY 14094
716.433.8405
www.niagaralanding.com

Palmer Vineyards
5120 Sound Avenue
Riverhead, NY 11901
631.722.9463
www.palmervineyards.com

Peconic Bay Winery
31320 Main Road, PO Box 818
Cutchogue, NY 11935
631.734.7361
www.peconicbaywinery.com

Penguin Bay
Winery and Champagne House
6075 Route 414
Hector, NY 14841
315.549.8326
www.penguinbaywinery.com

Pindar Vineyards
591 A Bicycle Path
Peconic, NY 11776
631.734.6200
www.pindar.net

Raphael
39390 Main Road
Peconic, NY 11958
631.765.1100
www.raphaelwine.com

Rooster Hill Vineyards
489 Route 54 South
Penn Yan, NY 14527
315.536.4773
www.roosterhilll.com

Seneca Shore Wine Cellars
929 Davy Road
Penn Yan, NY 14527
315.536.0882
www.SenecaWine.com

Sherwood House Vineyards
2600 Oregon Road
Mattituck, NY 11952
631.298.1396
www.sherwoodhousevineyards.com

Standing Stone Vineyards
9934 Route 414
Hector, NY 14841
607.582.6051
www.standingstonewines.com

Stoutridge Vineyard
10 Ann Kaley Lane
Marlboro, NY 12542
845.236.7620
www.stoutridge.com

Swedish Hill Winery
4565 State Route 414
Romulus, NY 14541
315.549.8326
www.swedishhill.com

Ventosa Vineyards
3440 Route 96A
Geneva, NY 14456
315.719.0000
www.ventosavineyards.com

Vetter Vineyards Winery
8005 Prospect Station Road
Westfield, NY 14787
716.326.3100
www.vettervineyards.com

Wagner Vineyards
9322 State Route 414
Lodi, NY 14860
607.582.6450
www.wagnervineyards.com

Warwick Valley Winery & Distillery
114 Little York Road
Warwick, NY 10990
845.258.4858
www.wvwinery.com

White Springs Farm Estate Winery
4200 Route 14 South
Geneva, NY 14456
315.781.9463
www.whitespringswinery.com

The Winery at Marjim Manor
7171 East Lake Road
Appleton, NY 14008
716.778.7001
www.MarjimManor.com

Wölffer Estate Vineyard
139 Sagg Road / PO Box 9002
Sagaponack, NY 11962
631.537.5106
www.wolffer.com